☦

THE HOLY PSALTER

THE PSALTER

According to the Seventy

Of Saint David the Prophet and King

Together with the Nine Odes
And an Interpretation of How the Psalter
Should be Recited Throughout the Whole Year

Translated from the Greek Septuagint by the
HOLY TRANSFIGURATION MONASTERY
BOSTON, MASSACHUSETTS
2022

Copyright © 1974 by the
Holy Transfiguration Monastery, Brookline, Massachusetts 02445
All rights reserved. Any copying or distribution by any means
without prior written permission is forbidden.
Printed in Canada
Library of Congress Catalogue Number: 74-76941
ISBN 10: 0-943405-00-9
ISBN 13: 978-0-943405-00-1
First Printing 1974, 3,000 copies
Second Printing 1987, 3,000 copies
Third Printing 1997, 5,000 copies
[Pocket Edition 2007, 5,000 copies]
Fourth Printing 2008, 5,000 copies
[Pocket Edition, Second Printing, 2010, 10,000 copies]
[Pocket Edition, Third Printing, 2020, 10,000 copies]
Fifth Printing 2022, 5,000 copies

IN MEMORIAM

PANAGIOTIS ZACHARIS

OF BOSTON, MASSACHUSETTS

1940–2008

JOANNA LAM

OF QUINCY, MASSACHUSETTS

1955–2022

CHRIST PANTOCRATOR
By Photios Kontoglou

FOREWORD

In the Name of the Father, the Son, and the Holy Spirit.

*Blessed is the people
that knoweth jubilation.
Psalm 88:14*

BLESSED, truly, and thrice blessed are the people that know jubilation. And this people is the holy nation, the royal priesthood, the people for His own possession of whom the Holy Apostle Peter speaks (cf. I Peter 2:9), in short, the beloved Israel which is made up of the Apostles, Prophets, Patriarchs, Martyrs, Hierarchs, Righteous Fathers and Mothers and all rightly believing Orthodox Christians. Verily, we are that Chosen People which in time past were not a people, but are now the people of God: which had not obtained mercy, but now have obtained mercy (cf. I Peter 2:10), that we should show forth the praises of Him Who hath called us out of darkness into His wondrous light (cf. I Peter 2:9).

And from olden times Israel has declared the praises of our true God with psalms and hymns found in that book of the Old Testament called the "Psalter." Our Saviour Himself and the Holy Apostles used them and chanted them (cf. Mark 14:26). Therefore, it was only natural that the first Christians from the nations who were grafted onto the stock of Israel should have prayed with the same voice as the fathers of old. Actually, the first services of the Church in New Testament times were composed almost exclusively from the psalms, which were chanted in the Hebraic manner in the translation used for generations by the Hebrews in the diaspora, the Septuagint. Till this day, there is no service of the Church which is not replete with psalms: the Hours, Vespers, Compline, Matins, even the Divine Liturgy itself; all begin and end with psalms. The *prokeimena* for Vespers and for the lections from the Epistles in the Liturgy, and the introits at the Little Entrance are all from the Psalter. In short, the psalms serve as the framework for all our Church services, and it is around this framework that, through the centuries, the other hymns and odes have been added.

So much are the psalms employed in the worship of the Church that, in Greek, the word to chant is properly ψάλλω—to sing a psalm; and the word for chanter is ψάλτης—a psalmist.

Again and again in the services, references are made to the psalms, and David is called upon to bear witness to the feast with his verses. Occasionally in icons of the Great Feasts, David is depicted in some corner or shown leaning out of a tower, or from a wall in the background, with a scroll in his hand proclaiming a verse from the Psalter proper to the feast. In the Matins service for the Holy Theophany of our Lord, we hear in the Ninth Ode:

> O David, come in the Spirit to them that are enlightened, and do thou sing: Draw nigh now unto God with faith, and be ye enlightened. For this poor man cried—even Adam in his fall—and the Lord heard him; for He is come, and in the streams of the Jordan, He hath made new him who was corrupted. (cf. Ps. 33:5–6)

And in Matins for the Feast of the Dormition of the All-holy Theotokos, the first *kathisma* reads:

> David, raise thy voice and cry: What is this present feast today? This is she whom I extolled with hymns and praises in the Psalms as Child of God and as Daughter and as a Virgin; and Christ, Who seedlessly was born of her pure womb, hath translated her unto the mansions beyond. For this cause mothers and young daughters and brides of Christ all cry out with joy: Rejoice, O thou who hast been translated to the Kingdom of Heaven. (cf. Psalm 44)

Every detail of the voluntary Passion and the Resurrection of our Saviour is hymned during the compunctionate services of Holy Week and the Great and Glorious Pascha with verses taken from the psalms. Then again, the whole Psalter is read during the Vespers and Matins services each week in twenty *kathismata*. During the Holy and Great Lent, the *kathismata* are doubled each day, and the Psalter is read through twice each week. Whole psalms and verses selected from the psalms are chanted for the *polyeleos* during the Matins service of a Vigil. The funeral service contains the whole of Psalm 118 divided into three *stases* in three tones. This is still chanted in monasteries for the funeral service and for the full memorial service. Thus one can justly claim that in our sacred services, the Psalter is the most used book of Holy Writ. And when one either chants in congregation, or hears the psalms chanted in the manner that they have been chanted from the beginning by the Church, monophonically and antiphonically, that person knows that we are truly that well-beloved Israel, the blessed people that knows jubilation.

Of old, many monastics learned the Psalter by heart, and there is an ancient local canon which required that those who were to be consecrated bishops should know the Psalter from memory. Many are those Orthodox Christians, monastics and lay-people, even among the most illiterate peasants, who know many of the psalms by heart, especially those that are chanted again and again in church, those from the *typica* and the *polyeleos,* Psalm 50, and others. Psalm 102, chanted at the beginning of the Liturgy, is the most tender and comforting psalm. How blessed it would be if the English-speaking Orthodox followed this soul-profiting example and learned to recite and chant, if not the entire Psalter, at least some of the more frequently used psalms!

Seeing, therefore, the need for a good English translation of the Church Psalter which could be used liturgically, we have laboured for many years now seeking to achieve a translation both poetic and as close to the original as possible. This present translation is the reapings of our labours and pains.

We made one addition to the second printing of the Psalter. When an Orthodox Christian has reposed, it is traditional to read the entire Psalter over him during the wake which precedes the funeral. There is a special prayer recited on his behalf at the end of each *kathisma.* This prayer may be found on page 263.

First and foremost we thank our true God Who has allowed us sinners to undertake this holy labour, and secondly, all those pious souls who have contributed to bring about its publication through prayers, especially the handmaid of God Joanna, through whose generosity this printing was made possible.

Remember us also, beloved brethren, fellow pilgrims and sojourners in this conversation here below, and pray that we find mercy in the Day of the Lord.

HOLY TRANSFIGURATION MONASTERY

Glory be to God for all things. Amen. Amen. Amen.

Holy and Great Lent, 2022

TRANSLATORS' INTRODUCTION

As an English-speaking, Orthodox Christian community of monastics planted here in the New World, we, perhaps more than others, have felt an acute need for a translation of the Book of Psalms. The Holy Psalter is the main inspiration for our divine services. In fact, there is not a service of the Church which does not bear the distinct imprint of these "songs of Sion." Hence, it became immediately clear to us that, without a translation of the Church's Psalter, any other translation of the holy services would be, at best, tentative.

From the very beginning, the Septuagint was the version of the Old Testament which was used by the Christian Church. This is attested to, not only by the early Patristic writings and ancient Christian hymnology, but also by the New Testament itself. With very few exceptions, the Apostles and Evangelists used the Septuagint when quoting the Old Testament. This is not surprising; for — according to one tradition widely accepted by the ancient Jewish community and by many of the Fathers — the Septuagint translation had been made by two and *seventy* (hence its name) pious Hebrew scholars in Alexandria, and was the universally accepted translation used by those of the Jewish faith, both within the Holy Land and throughout the diaspora.

This too is not surprising. For aside from the fact that the Jews themselves no longer spoke Hebrew, the Hebrew text itself presented certain difficulties. For one thing, in Ancient Hebrew, the written texts omitted the vowels. And as Fr. Lazarus Moore points out in the introduction to his translation of the *Holy Psalter,* "it is easy to see that a word like *brd* could be rendered bread, bird, bard, brayed, broad, beard, bored, breed, brood, braid, bride, bred, buried." As a result, textual variations were almost inescapable.

What is equally important is the fact that the present day Hebrew version (also known as the Massoretic text) is itself the result of a doctrinal upheaval which shook Judaism early in the ninth century A.D. During this time, a sharp controversy broke out between the Rabbinical scholars and the Karaite sect (the Hebrew form of the name is *Beni Miqra*, "Sons of Reading," i.e., of the Scriptures). As W. O. E. Oesterley notes in his work *The Psalms:*

> The Karaites undertook a most minute and critical study of the Biblical text; and in order to oppose and refute the Karaite teaching, the Rabbis had to undertake a similar task. This dual critical study developed into a very keen contest between the Rabbinical and Karaite champions; and there is no doubt that the bulk of the work . . . must be assigned to the heretical Karaites. (ibid. p. 114)

As a result, in his critical edition of the Hebrew Psalter, Oesterley time and time again comes to the conclusion that, in a countless number of verses, the Massoretic text is, as he puts it, "hopelessly corrupt," and the Septuagint is repeatedly called upon in the author's effort to shed some light on what the original Hebrew rendering may have once been.

This does not mean that the Septuagint has itself remained immune to variations or errors that have crept in over the years. Indeed, centuries of diverse recensions and scribal errors have bequeathed us some variants of the Greek Old Testament, especially as regards the Book of Daniel. In the Septuagint Psalter, however, the textual differences are slight, as Alfred Rahlfs bears witness in his critical edition of the translation of the Seventy. Therefore, it is no surprise also that in none of the printed Psalters (including the critical editions) did we find a uniformity in either verse enumeration or verse division. The punctuation and division of the text into verses, and the enumeration of the verses themselves, are, in any case, the work of editors of a relatively recent date.

On the other hand, it was gratifying to see that Rahlfs' edition, the best of non-Orthodox Christian critical editions of the Septuagint, attests to the accuracy and careful scholarship of the best of the Orthodox Church's printed texts of the Greek Old Testament, i.e. the famous Moscow Edition of 1821. The Moscow Edition has been acclaimed by scholars and pious laymen alike. The fathers of Mount Athos have long borne witness to the accuracy of this particular edition, and we here at the monastery were fortunate enough to have two copies at our disposal for the work of translation. What is truly lamentable, and indeed inexcusable, is the fact that the modern editions published in Greece—where countless theologians and scholars of the Greek language are readily available—are so replete with errors, including mis-spellings, and the repetition, misplacement or even total omission of whole verses. This too has made us come to appreciate the value of the Moscow Edition.

To date, there exist two published translations of the Septuagint Old Testament into English, that of the Falcon Press and that of Bagster's Publishing House. Of these, the first has two major drawbacks: (1) with few exceptions, the translation is very poor and, (2) the Books included and their arrangement are based on the Protestant canon. The Bagster's edition is very much superior, in that the translation is quite excellent and, in addition, all the Books of the Old Testament are included. One drawback to this edition is its erratic arrangement of the Books of the canon, and one other major fault is that it is based, not on the Received Text, but primarily on one codex only.

Then in 1966, an English translation of the Holy Psalter was published by Fr. Lazarus Moore in Madras, India. On hearing this, we were overjoyed, for we knew of the excellent work that Fr. Lazarus had already done in translating *The Ladder of Divine Ascent*, *The Arena*, the lives of Saints and many Church services. Although we had already done much work on the Psalter, we thought and hoped that now, with the publication of Fr. Moore's translation, we would at least be spared the great expense of publishing it ourselves. However, we were greatly disappointed in that the Nine Odes were not included in Fr. Moore's publication, as they should be in every Orthodox Psalter. Also, the style of language was not, properly speaking, liturgical, and was therefore more suitable for personal use (e.g. in Psalm 78, Fr. Lazarus has the psalmist cry out, "... they have defiled Thy holy temple; they have made Jerusalem like a vegetable dump"). In addition, and more important from a doctrinal point of view, we found serious omissions in the text itself; for example in Psalm 67:19, the words "Thou leddest captivity captive" are omitted. Since this is an extremely important Messianic text concerning Our Saviour's trampling down of death by death, we could not possibly imagine that Fr. Lazarus would have deleted it purposely. We could attribute it only to poor proofreading. However, we learned from Fr. Lazarus himself that he was responsible for the proofreading and that, in fact, he had caught many errors which the printers refused to correct! This, together with the realization that English is not the spoken language of India and the fact that Fr. Lazarus had to work alone and that his economic and textual resources were extremely limited, make his contribution a truly heroic one. The work of translating a book such as the Holy Psalter is difficult enough to begin with; taking into consideration the conditions under which Fr. Lazarus was forced to work, it is practically impossible. Nevertheless, Fr. Lazarus' translation is a valuable one which can give one new insights into many psalmic passages.

In addition to the above, we had in manuscript form a translation of the Holy Psalter executed by Fr. Michael Gelsinger of Buffalo, New York. Fr. Gelsinger's contribution to the amount of Orthodox Catholic liturgical material available in English is voluminous and monumental. Already, over two generations of Orthodox Christians have been spiritually enlightened and edified by the untiring efforts of this man. His knowledge of Greek, coupled with a superb command of the English tongue, as well as his poetic gift and musical talent, have inspired countless Orthodox Christian souls.

Fr. Gelsinger's translation of the Holy Psalter was by far the best that we had encountered. One of its principle advantages is that the Greek word order is employed whenever the translator wishes to give special emphasis and strength to a given verse. On the other hand, its major drawbacks are a lack of uniformity in style (e.g. in one instance, he uses the older verbal form, such as "bringeth," and in other places, he lapses into the more modern form, "brings"). Also, Fr. Gelsinger's training was primarily in Classical Greek, whereas the Greek of the Septuagint, with its heavily Hebraic idioms, is a very different language. As a result, many constructions escaped Fr. Gelsinger which would not have escaped another who had read the Greek Psalter throughout his life. For example, understanding the word in its classical sense, Fr. Gelsinger translates καλὸν as "beautiful" (as in Psalm 132:1). However, in *Koine*, the Greek of the Septuagint and the New Testament, καλὸν no longer means "beautiful" primarily, but "good." If such were not the case, Our Saviour's words in Luke 14:34, «καλὸν τὸ ἅλας...» ("Salt is good...") would make no sense. We are nevertheless very much indebted to his work, which was a great well-spring of inspiration for us, and our present text reflects this.

As for the basic principles which guided us in the present work, the following can be said. In the matter of capitalisation, we followed the example of the Greek and Slavonic Psalters. If, for example, the word "king" clearly referred to God or to the Messiah, it was capitalised. There where it might refer to the kings of Judea as well, it was left uncapitalised. The word «Χριστὸς» was rendered "Christ" whenever the text was clearly messianic, and "anointed one" wherever it might also refer to the kings of Judea or some others as well. The spelling of all proper names was based on the Septuagint rendering (e.g. "Sion" instead of "Zion"). It might be mentioned here that such was the case with all English translations of the Holy Scriptures until the end of the nineteenth century.

Wherever possible, we strove to preserve the distinctly Hebraic idiom and imagery of the Septuagint. In Psalm 67, for example, the vision of the "butter mountain" rises before us. In the Septuagint, the phrase here is πίον ὄρος. Speaking literally, πίον means "rich" or "fat," and is used especially with reference to rich, thick milk or cream. Although a very ancient word, βούτυρον (literally "cow cheese"), exists for "butter," the term πίον is used also when referring to the fat of an animal, and especially the fat in a sheep's tail, which, in Palestine, is considered a great delicacy and is used as a spread on bread in much the same way as we use butter. We believe the phrase "butter mountain" appropriately describes the image of a rich, fertile land, which the other renderings (e.g. "rich mountain" or "mountain of curds") fail to convey. Bagster's edition also misses the point in this verse by rendering it "a rich mountain, a swelling mountain." However, in a footnote, the translators explain that the Greek term τετυρομένον means literally "curdled like cheese," and not "swelling" as they have it. In contrast, the phrase, "a butter mountain, a curdled mountain," gives us a much more accurate picture of the Psalmist's image. And indeed, what greater delight could there be for a formerly nomadic people who dreamt of a land "that flowed with milk and honey," than to have "the mountain of God, a butter mountain" rising in their midst? And since many Fathers have taken this passage as an image of the Mother of God, what greater delight, indeed, could there be for the New Israel, the "race of Christians," than to have this grace-filled "mountain of God," this rich and fertile "butter mountain" rising in our midst?

An outstanding example of the difficulties which translators confront is the word ἐξομολογέομαι. The primary sense of the word in antiquity was and still is "to confess" or "admit" one's misdeeds or sins. Later, it came also to mean "to profess," then "to acknowledge," "to make grateful acknowledgements," then "to give thanks" or "to give praise." In short, it acquired all these meanings without losing any of its former definitions. How to translate such a word? Obviously, no single English word encompasses all these nuances.

The only solution left to us was to choose the definition which fitted the text in each instance, both from a doctrinal and a poetical point of view.

We have purposely chosen a style of English following that of the King James version, not only because it is of a more liturgical nature, but also because it is a more ancient and purer form of the language. This, too, contributes to its solemnity and beauty. By this choice, we have avoided many of the compromises and inconsistencies in style of the more recent translations.

Acknowledgements are due to the late Mr. G. E. H. Palmer of Berkshire, England, co-translator of the English *Philokalia,* and also to the theologian and scholar, Fr. Michael Azkoul of St. Louis, Missouri, for their valuable advice and observations regarding the renderings of many passages.

Unto Almighty God we offer up thanks that He has counted us, the unworthy, worthy of presenting this translation to the Orthodox faithful, that His holy Name might thereby be praised and glorified.

> In congregations bless ye God,
> the Lord from the well-springs of Israel.
> *Psalm 67:27*

FROM THE FATHERS

On the Psalms

I F we keep vigil in church, David comes first, last, and central. If early in the morning we want songs and hymns, first, last, and central is David again. If we are occupied with the funeral solemnities of those who have fallen asleep, or if the virgins sit at home and spin, David is first, last, and central. O amazing wonder! Many who have made little progress in literature know the Psalter by heart. Nor is it only in cities and churches that David is famous; in the village market, in the desert, and in uninhabitable land, he excites the praise of God. In monasteries, among those holy choirs of angelic armies, David is first, last, and central. In the convents of virgins, where there are the communities of those who imitate Mary, in the deserts where there are men crucified to the world, who live their life in heaven with God, David is first, last, and central. All other men at night are overcome by sleep; David alone is active, and gathering the servants of God into seraphic bands, he turns earth into heaven, and converts men into angels.

Saint John Chrysostom

W HEN, indeed, the Holy Spirit saw that the human race was guided only with difficulty toward virtue, and that, because of our inclination toward pleasure, we were neglectful of an upright life, what did He do? The delight of melody He mingled with the doctrines so that by the pleasantness and softness of the sound heard we might receive without perceiving it the benefit of the words, just as wise physicians who, when giving the fastidious rather bitter drugs to drink, frequently smear the cup with honey. Therefore, He devised for us these harmonious melodies of the psalms, that they who are children in age, or even those who are youthful in disposition, might to all appearances chant, but in reality, become trained in soul. For, never has any one of the many indifferent persons gone away easily holding in mind either an apostolic or prophetic message, but they do chant the words of the psalms, even in the home, and they spread them around in the market place, and, if perchance, someone becomes exceedingly wrathful, when he begins to be soothed by the psalm, he departs with the wrath immediately lulled to sleep by means of the melody.

A psalm implies serenity of soul; it is the author of peace, which calms bewildering and seething thoughts. For, it softens the wrath of the soul, and what is unbridled it chastens. A psalm forms friendships, unites those separated, conciliates those at enmity. Who, indeed, can still consider as an enemy him with whom he has uttered the same prayer to God? So that psalmody, bringing about choral singing, a bond, as it were, toward unity, and joining people into a harmonious union of one choir, produces also the greatest of blessings, love. A psalm is a city of refuge from the demons; a means of inducing help from the angels, a weapon in fears by night, a rest from the toils of the day, a safeguard for infants, an adornment for those at the height of their vigour, a consolation for the elders, a most fitting ornament for women. It peoples the solitudes; it rids the market places of excesses; it is the elementary exposition of beginners, the improvement of those advancing, the solid support of the perfect, the voice of the Church. It brightens feast days; it creates a sorrow which is in accordance with God. For, a psalm calls forth a tear even from a heart of stone. A psalm is the work of angels, a heavenly institution, the spiritual incense.

Saint Basil the Great

PAMBO, our holy father, being an illiterate man went to one of the fathers who knew letters for the purpose of being taught a psalm. And, having heard the first verse of the thirty-eighth psalm, "I said: I will take heed to my ways lest I sin with my tongue," he departed without staying to hear the second verse, saying, "this one will suffice if I can learn it in deed." And when the father who had given him the verse reproved him because he had not seen him for the space of six months, the blessed one answered that he had not yet learned in deed the verse of the psalm. After a considerable lapse of time, being asked by one of his friends whether he had made himself master of the verse, he answered thus, "In all of nineteen years, I have only just succeeded in accomplishing it."

From the Ecclesiastical History
of Socrates Scholasticus

VERSES
TO THE DIVINE DAVID

Be silent, Orpheus; thy lyre throw aside, O Hermes.
The tripod at Delphi hath sunk into oblivion for evermore.
For us David doth now play the Spirit's lyre,
The hidden things of God's mysteries he revealeth;
A multitude of ancient wonders he narrateth;
Of the Creator of creation, doth he move one to sing.
Saving all those men he initiateth, as he writeth his verses,
Sinners doth he bring to desire repentance.
Among other teachings, to the throng doth he declare the Judge's judgments.
The purging, he doth teach, of soulful sinnings.

A COUPLET
TO THE SAME

The Psalter of David, whose sayings are as stones,
Doth crush the passions as they were another Goliath.

THE SONG OF DAVID THE PROPHET AND KING

THE FIRST KATHISMA

PSALM I. I

David's. Without superscription among the Hebrews.

BLESSED IS THE MAN that hath not walked in the counsel of the ungodly, nor stood in the way of sinners, nor sat in the seat of the pestilent.

But his will is rather in the law of the Lord, and in His law will he meditate day and night.

And he shall be like the tree which is planted by the streams of the waters, which shall bring forth its fruit in its season; and its leaf shall not fall, and all things whatsoever he may do shall prosper.

Not so are the ungodly, not so; but rather they are like the chaff which the wind doth hurl away from the face of the earth.

For this reason shall the ungodly not stand up in judgment, nor sinners in the council of the righteous.

For the Lord knoweth the way of the righteous, and the way of the ungodly shall perish.

PSALM II. 2

A psalm of David.

WHY have the heathen raged, and the peoples meditated empty things?

The kings of the earth were aroused, and the rulers were assembled together, against the Lord, and against His Christ.

Let us break their bonds asunder, and let us cast away their yoke from us.

He that dwelleth in the heavens shall laugh them to scorn, and the Lord shall deride them.

5 Then shall He speak unto them in His wrath, and in His anger shall He trouble them.

But as for Me, I was established as king by Him, upon Sion His holy mountain, proclaiming the commandment of the Lord.

The Lord said unto Me: Thou art My Son, this day have I begotten Thee.

Ask of Me, and I will give Thee the nations for Thine inheritance, and the uttermost parts of the earth for Thy possession.

Thou shalt herd them with a rod of iron; Thou shalt shatter them like a potter's vessels.

10 And now, O ye kings, understand; be instructed, all ye that judge the earth.

Serve ye the Lord with fear, and rejoice in Him with trembling.

Lay hold of instruction, lest at any time the Lord be angry, and ye perish from the righteous way.

When quickly His wrath be kindled, blessed are all that have put their trust in Him.

PSALM III. 3

*A psalm of David, when he fled from the face
of Abessalom his son, in the wilderness.*

O LORD, why are they multiplied that afflict me? Many rise up against me.

Many say unto my soul: There is no salvation for him in his God.

But Thou, O Lord, art my helper, my glory, and the lifter up of my head.

I cried unto the Lord with my voice, and He heard me out of His holy mountain.

I laid me down and slept; I awoke, for the Lord will help me.

I will not be afraid of ten thousands of people that set themselves against me round about.

Arise, O Lord, save me, O my God, for Thou hast smitten all who without cause are mine enemies; the teeth of sinners hast Thou broken.

Salvation is of the Lord, and Thy blessing is upon Thy people.

> Glory. Both now. Alleluia.

PSALM IV. 4

For the end: an ode of David among the psalms.

WHEN I called upon Thee, O God of my righteousness, Thou didst hearken unto me; in mine affliction Thou hast enlarged me.

Have compassion on me and hear my prayer.

O ye sons of men, how long will ye be slow of heart? Why do ye love vanity, and seek after falsehood?

Know also that the Lord hath made wondrous His

holy one; the Lord will hearken unto me when I cry unto Him.

5 Be angry, and sin not; feel compunction upon your beds for what ye say in your hearts.

Sacrifice a sacrifice of righteousness, and hope in the Lord. Many say: Who will show unto us good things?

The light of Thy countenance, O Lord, hath been signed upon us; Thou hast given gladness to my heart.

From the fruit of their wheat, wine, and oil are they multiplied.

In peace in the same place I shall lay me down and sleep.

10 For Thou, O Lord, alone hast made me to dwell in hope.

PSALM V. 5

For the end: a psalm of David for her that obtained the inheritance.

UNTO my words give ear, O Lord; hear my cry. Attend unto the voice of my supplication, O my King and my God; for unto Thee will I pray, O Lord.

In the morning Thou shalt hear my voice. In the morning shall I stand before Thee, and Thou shalt look upon me; for not a God that willest iniquity art Thou.

He that worketh evil shall not dwell near Thee, nor shall transgressors abide before Thine eyes.

Thou hast hated all them that work iniquity; Thou shalt destroy all them that speak a lie.

5 A man that is bloody and deceitful shall the Lord abhor.

But as for me, in the multitude of Thy mercy shall I go

into Thy house; I shall worship toward Thy holy temple in fear of Thee.

O Lord, guide me in the way of Thy righteousness; because of mine enemies, make straight my way before Thee,

For in their mouth there is no truth; their heart is vain.

Their throat is an open sepulchre, with their tongues have they spoken deceitfully; judge them, O God.

10 Let them fall down on account of their own devisings; according to the multitude of their ungodliness, cast them out, for they have embittered Thee, O Lord.

And let all them be glad that hope in Thee; they shall ever rejoice, and Thou shalt dwell among them.

And all shall glory in Thee that love Thy Name, for Thou shalt bless the righteous.

O Lord, as with a shield of Thy good pleasure hast Thou crowned us.

PSALM VI. 6

For the end: a psalm of David among the hymns for the eighth.

O LORD, rebuke me not in Thine anger, nor chasten me in Thy wrath.

Have mercy on me, O Lord, for I am weak. Heal me, O Lord, for my bones are troubled, and my soul is troubled greatly; but Thou, O Lord, how long?

Turn to me again, O Lord, deliver my soul; save me for Thy mercy's sake.

For in death there is none that is mindful of Thee, and in hades who will confess Thee?

5   I toiled in my groaning; every night I will wash my bed, with tears will I water my couch.

Through wrath is mine eye become troubled, I have grown old among all mine enemies.

Depart from me, all ye that work vanity, for the Lord hath heard the voice of my weeping.

The Lord hath heard my supplication, the Lord hath received my prayer.

Let all mine enemies be greatly put to shame and be troubled, let them be turned back, and speedily be greatly put to shame.

Glory. Both now. Alleluia.

PSALM VII. 7

A psalm of David, which he sang unto the Lord concerning the words of Chusi, the son of Jemeni.

O LORD my God, in Thee have I put my hope; save me from them that persecute me, and do Thou deliver me.

Lest at any time like a lion he seize my soul, when there is none to redeem me, nor to save.

O Lord my God, if I have done this, if there be injustice in my hands,

If I have paid back evil to them that rendered evil unto me, then let me fall back empty from mine enemies.

5   Then let the enemy pursue my soul, and take it, and let him tread down my life into the earth, and my glory let him bring down into the dust.

Arise, O Lord, in Thine anger, exalt Thyself to the furthest boundaries of Thine enemies.

And arouse Thyself, O Lord my God, in the commandment which Thou hast enjoined, and a congregation of peoples shall surround Thee. And for their sakes return Thou on high.

The Lord shall judge the peoples. Judge me, O Lord, according to my righteousness, and according to mine innocence within me.

Let the wickedness of sinners be ended, and do Thou guide the righteous man, O God, that searchest out the hearts and reins.

Righteous is my help from God, Who saveth them who are upright of heart.

God is a judge that is righteous, strong and forbearing, and inflicteth not wrath every day.

Unless ye be converted, His glittering sword shall He furbish; He hath bent His bow, and hath made it ready.

And on it He hath made ready the instruments of death, His arrows for them that rage hotly hath He perfected.

Behold, he was in travail with unrighteousness, he hath conceived toil and brought forth iniquity.

He opened a pit and dug it, and he shall fall into the hole which he hath made.

His toil shall return upon his own head, and upon his own pate shall his unrighteousness come down.

I will give praise unto the Lord according to His righteousness, and I will chant unto the Name of the Lord Most High.

PSALM VIII. 8

For the end: a psalm of David concerning the wine-presses.

O LORD, our Lord, how wonderful is Thy Name in all the earth! For Thy magnificence is lifted high above the heavens.

Out of the mouths of babes and sucklings hast Thou perfected praise, because of Thine enemies, to destroy the enemy and avenger.

For I will behold the heavens, the works of Thy fingers, the moon and the stars, which Thou hast founded.

What is man, that Thou art mindful of him? Or the son of man, that Thou visitest him?

Thou hast made him a little lower than the angels; with glory and honour hast Thou crowned him, and Thou hast set him over the works of Thy hands.

All things hast Thou subjected under his feet, sheep, and all oxen, yea, and the beasts of the field,

The birds of the air, and the fish of the sea, the things that pass through the paths of the sea.

O Lord, our Lord, how wonderful is Thy Name in all the earth!

Glory. Both now. Alleluia.

THE SECOND KATHISMA

PSALM IX. 9

For the end: a psalm of David concerning the hidden things of the son.

I WILL confess Thee, O Lord, with my whole heart, I will tell of all Thy wonders.

I will be glad and rejoice in Thee, I will chant unto Thy Name, O Most High.

When mine enemy be turned back, they shall grow weak and shall perish before Thy face,

For Thou hast maintained my judgment and my cause; Thou hast sat upon a throne, O Thou that judgest righteousness.

Thou hast rebuked the heathen, and the ungodly man hath perished; his name Thou hast blotted out for ever, and unto ages of ages.

The swords of the enemy have utterly failed, and his cities Thou hast destroyed.

The remembrance of him hath perished with a resounding noise, but the Lord for ever abideth.

In judgment hath He prepared His throne, and He Himself will judge the world in righteousness; He will judge the peoples in uprightness.

And the Lord is become a refuge for the poor man, a helper in times of well-being and in afflictions.

And let them that know Thy Name hope in Thee, for Thou hast not forsaken them that seek Thee, O Lord.

Chant unto the Lord Who dwelleth in Sion, proclaim ye His ways among the nations.

For He that maketh enquiry for blood hath remembered them, He hath not forgotten the cry of the paupers.

Have mercy on me, O Lord; see my humiliation which I have suffered from mine enemies, O Thou that dost raise me up from the gates of death,

That I may declare all Thy praises in the gates of the daughter of Sion. We will rejoice in Thy salvation.

15 The heathen are ensnared in the destruction which they have wrought; in this snare which they hid hath their foot been caught.

The Lord is known by the judgments which He executeth; in the works of his own hands hath the sinner been caught.

Let sinners be turned away unto hades, yea, all the nations that are forgetful of God.

For the poor man shall not be forgotten to the end; the patience of the paupers shall not perish for ever.

Arise, O Lord, let not man prevail; let the nations be judged before Thee.

20 O Lord, set a lawgiver over them; let the heathen know that they are but men.

Why, O Lord, hast Thou gone to stand afar off? Why dost Thou overlook us in times of well-being and in afflictions?

When the ungodly man is arrogant, the poor man burneth within; they are caught in the counsels which they devise.

For the sinner praiseth himself in the lusts of his soul, and the unrighteous man likewise blesseth himself therein.

The sinner hath provoked the Lord; according to the magnitude of his wrath, he careth not; God is not before him.

25 Profane are his ways in every season, Thy judgments are removed from his sight, over all his enemies shall he gain dominion.

For he said in his heart: I shall not be shaken; from generation to generation shall I be without harm.

With cursing is his mouth filled, and with bitterness and deceit; under his tongue are toil and travail.

He sitteth in ambush with the rich in secret places, that he may slay the innocent; his eyes are set upon the poor man.

He lieth in wait in a secret place like a lion in his den; he lieth in wait to seize upon the poor man, to seize upon the poor man when he draweth him in.

30 In his snare will he humble himself, he will bow down and fall while gaining dominion over the poor.

For he said in his heart: God hath forgotten; He hath turned away His face, that He might not see unto the end.

Arise, O Lord my God, let Thy hand be lifted high; forget not Thy paupers to the end.

Why hath the ungodly one provoked God? For he hath said in his heart: He will not make enquiry.

Thou seest, for Thou understandest travail and anger, that Thou mightest deliver him into Thy hands. To Thee hath the beggar been abandoned; for the orphan art Thou a helper.

35 Break Thou the arm of the sinner and of the evil man; his sin shall be sought out and be found no more.

The Lord shall be king for ever, and unto the ages of ages. Ye heathen shall perish out of His land.

The desire of the poor hast Thou heard, O Lord; to the preparation of their heart hath Thine ear been attentive,

To judge for the orphan and the humble, that man may no more presume to be haughty upon the earth.

PSALM X. 10

For the end: a psalm of David.

In the Lord have I hoped; how will ye say to my soul: Flee unto the mountains like a sparrow?

For behold, the sinners have bent their bow, they have prepared arrows for the quiver, to shoot down in a moonless night the upright of heart.

For what Thou hast formed they have destroyed; and the righteous man, what hath he done?

The Lord is in His holy temple; the Lord, in heaven is His throne; His eyes are set upon the poor man, His eyelids examine the sons of men.

The Lord examineth the righteous man and the ungodly; but he that loveth unrighteousness hateth his own soul.

He will rain down snares upon sinners; fire and brimstone and wind of tempest shall be the portion of their cup.

For the Lord is righteous and hath loved righteousness; upon uprightness hath His countenance looked.

Glory. Both now. Alleluia.

PSALM XI. 11

For the end: a psalm of David for the eighth.

SAVE me, O Lord, for a righteous man there is no more; for truths have diminished from the sons of men.

Vain things hath each man spoken to his neighbour; deceitful lips are in his heart, and in his heart hath he spoken evils.

Let the Lord destroy all deceitful lips and the tongue that speaketh boastful words, which have said:

Our tongue will we magnify, our lips are our own. Who is lord over us?

5 Because of the distress of the beggars and the groaning of the poor, now will I arise, saith the Lord; I will establish them in salvation, I will be manifest therein.

The words of the Lord are pure words, silver that is fired, tried in the earth, brought to sevenfold purity.

Thou, O Lord, shalt keep us and shalt preserve us from this generation, and for evermore.

The ungodly walk round about; to the measure of Thy loftiness hast Thou esteemed the sons of men.

PSALM XII. 12

For the end: a psalm of David.

How long, O Lord, wilt Thou utterly forget me? How long wilt Thou turn Thy face away from me?

How long shall I take counsel in my soul with grievings in my heart by day and by night? How long shall mine enemy be exalted over me?

Look upon me, hear me, O Lord my God; enlighten mine eyes, lest at any time I sleep unto death.

Lest at any time mine enemy say: I have prevailed against him.

They that afflict me will rejoice if I am shaken; but as for me, I have hoped in Thy mercy. My heart will rejoice in Thy salvation.

I will sing unto the Lord, Who is my benefactor, and I will chant unto the Name of the Lord Most High.

PSALM XIII. 13

For the end: a psalm of David.

THE fool hath said in his heart: There is no God.

They are become corrupt and loathsome in their ways; there is none that doeth good, no not one.

The Lord looked down from heaven upon the sons of men, to see if there be any that understand or seek after God.

They are all gone astray, they are altogether rendered useless, there is none that doeth good, no not one.

Shall not all they that work iniquity come to understanding? They that eat up my people as they eat bread have not called upon the Lord.

There have they feared with fear where there is no fear; for the Lord is in the generation of the righteous.

The counsel of the poor man have ye shamed, but the Lord is his hope.

Who shall give out of Sion the salvation of Israel? When the Lord hath turned back the captivity of His people, Jacob shall rejoice and Israel shall be glad.

Glory. Both now. Alleluia.

PSALM XIV. 14

A psalm of David.

O LORD, who shall abide in Thy tabernacle? and who shall dwell in Thy holy mountain?

He that walketh blameless and worketh righteousness, speaking truth in his heart,

Who hath not spoken deceitfully with his tongue, neither hath done evil to his neighbour, nor taken up a reproach against those near him.

In his sight he that worketh evil is set at nought, but he glorifieth them that fear the Lord. He giveth oath to his neighbour, and forsweareth not.

5 He hath not lent his money on usury, and hath not received bribes against the innocent. He that doeth these things shall never be shaken.

PSALM XV. 15

A pillar inscription of David.

KEEP me, O Lord, for in Thee have I hoped.

I said unto the Lord: Thou art my Lord; for of my goods, no need hast Thou.

In the saints that are in His earth hath the Lord been wondrous; He hath wrought all His desires in them.

Their infirmities increased; thereupon they hastened. *(Diapsalm)* I will not assemble their assemblies of blood, nor will I make remembrance of their names through my lips.

5 The Lord is the portion of mine inheritance and of my cup. Thou art He that restorest mine inheritance unto me.

Portions have fallen to me that are among the best, for mine inheritance is most excellent to me.

I will bless the Lord Who hath given me understanding; moreover, even till night have my reins instructed me.

I beheld the Lord ever before me, for He is at my right hand, that I might not be shaken.

Therefore did my heart rejoice and my tongue was glad; moreover, my flesh shall dwell in hope.

10 For Thou wilt not abandon my soul in hades, nor wilt Thou suffer Thy Holy One to see corruption.

Thou hast made known to me the ways of life, Thou wilt fill me with gladness with Thy countenance; delights are in Thy right hand for ever.

PSALM XVI. 16

A prayer of David.

HEARKEN, O Lord, unto my righteousness, attend unto my supplication. Give ear unto my prayer, which cometh not from deceitful lips.

From before Thy face let my judgment come forth, let mine eyes behold uprightness.

Thou hast proved my heart, Thou hast visited it in the night, Thou hast tried me by fire, and unrighteousness was not found in me.

That my mouth might not speak of the works of men, for the sake of the words of Thy lips have I kept the ways that are hard.

5 Set my footsteps in Thy paths, that my steps may not be shaken.

I have cried for Thou hast hearkened unto me, O God. Incline Thine ear unto me, and hearken unto my words.

Let Thy mercies be made wonderful, O Thou that savest them that hope in Thee.

From them that have resisted Thy right hand, keep me, O Lord, as the apple of Thine eye.

In the shelter of Thy wings wilt Thou shelter me, from the face of the ungodly which have oppressed me.

Mine enemies have surrounded my soul, they have enclosed themselves with their own fat, their mouth hath spoken pride.

They that cast me out have now encircled me, they have set their eyes to look askance on the earth.

They have taken me as might a lion ready for his prey, and as might a lion's whelp that dwelleth in hiding.

Arise, O Lord, overtake them and trip their heels; deliver my soul from ungodly men, Thy sword from the enemies of Thy hand.

O Lord, from Thy few do Thou separate them from the earth in their life; yea, with Thy hidden treasures hath their belly been filled.

They have satisfied themselves with swine and have left the remnants to their babes.

But as for me, in righteousness shall I appear before Thy face; I shall be filled when Thy glory is made manifest to me.

Glory. Both now. Alleluia.

THE THIRD KATHISMA

PSALM XVII. 17

*For the end, for the child of the Lord, David: what things he spake
unto the Lord, even the words of this ode, in the day wherein
the Lord delivered him out of the hands of all his enemies,
and out of the hand of Saul; and he said:*

I WILL love Thee, O Lord, my strength; the Lord is my foundation, and my refuge, and my deliverer.

My God is my helper, and I will hope in Him, my defender, and the horn of my salvation, and my helper.

With praise will I call upon the Name of the Lord, and from mine enemies shall I be saved.

The pangs of death surrounded me, and the torrents of iniquity sorely troubled me.

The pangs of hades encircled me, round about the snares of death have overtaken me.

And in mine affliction I called upon the Lord, and unto my God I cried; He heard my voice out of His holy temple, and my cry before Him shall enter into His ears.

And the earth shook and was made to tremble, and the foundations of the mountains were troubled and were shaken, because God was angry with them.

There went up smoke in His wrath, and fire from His countenance set all aflame; coals were kindled therefrom.

And He bowed the heavens and came down, and thick darkness was under His feet.

And He mounted upon cherubim and flew, He flew upon the wings of the winds.

And He made darkness His hiding place, His tabernacle round about Him, dark water in the clouds of the air.

From the far-shining radiance that was before Him there passed by clouds, hail and coals of fire.

And the Lord thundered out of heaven, and the Most High gave forth His voice.

And He sent forth His arrows, and scattered them; and lightnings He multiplied, and troubled them sorely.

15 And the well-springs of the waters were seen, and the foundations of the world were revealed at Thy rebuke, O Lord, at the on-breathing of the spirit of Thy wrath.

He sent from on high, and He took me; He received me out of many waters.

He will deliver me from mine enemies which are mighty and from them that hate me, for they are stronger than I.

They overtook me in the day of mine affliction, and the Lord became my firm support.

And He led me forth into a spacious place; He will deliver me, because He desired me.

20 And the Lord will recompense me according to my righteousness, and according to the purity of my hands will He recompense me.

For I have kept the ways of the Lord, and I have not acted impiously toward my God.

For all His judgments are before me, and His statutes departed not from me.

And I shall be blameless with Him, and I shall keep myself from mine iniquity.

And the Lord will reward me according to my righteousness, and according to the purity of my hands before His eyes.

With the holy man wilt Thou be holy, and with the innocent man wilt Thou be innocent.

And with the elect man wilt Thou be elect, and with the perverse wilt Thou be perverse.

For Thou wilt save a humble people, and Thou wilt humble the eyes of the arrogant.

For Thou wilt light my lamp, O Lord my God, Thou wilt enlighten my darkness.

For by Thee shall I be delivered from a host of robbers, and by my God shall I leap over a wall.

As for my God, blameless is His way; the words of the Lord are tried in the fire; defender is He of all that hope in Him.

For who is god, save the Lord? And who is god, save our God?

It is God, Who girded me with power, and hath made my path blameless,

Who maketh my feet like the feet of a hart, and setteth me upon high places,

Who teacheth my hands for war; and Thou madest mine arms a bow of brass.

And Thou gavest me the shield of salvation, and Thy right hand hath upheld me.

And Thine instruction hath corrected me even unto the end; yea, Thine instruction, the same will teach me.

Thou hast enlarged my steps under me, and the tracks of my feet are not weakened.

I shall pursue mine enemies and I shall overtake them, and I shall not turn back until they fail.

I shall greatly afflict them, and they shall not be able to stand; they shall fall under my feet.

For Thou hast girded me with power for war, in subjection under me hast Thou bound the feet of all them that rose up against me.

And Thou hast made mine enemies turn their back before me, and them that hate me hast Thou utterly destroyed.

They cried, and there was no saviour—even to the Lord, and He hearkened not to them.

And I will grind them fine as dust before the face of the wind; I will trample them down as mud in the streets.

Deliver me from the gainsaying of the people; Thou wilt set me at the head of nations.

A people which I knew not hath served me; no sooner than their ear had heard, they obeyed me.

Sons that are strangers have lied unto me; sons that are strangers have grown old, and they have limped away from their paths.

The Lord liveth, and blessed is my God, and let the God of my salvation be exalted.

O God Who givest avengement unto me and hast subdued peoples under me,

O my Deliverer from enemies which are prone to anger, from them that arise up against me wilt Thou lift me high; from the unrighteous man deliver me.

For this cause will I confess Thee among the nations, O Lord, and unto Thy Name will I chant.

It is He that magnifieth the salvation of His king and worketh mercy for His anointed, for David, and for his seed unto eternity.

Glory. Both now. Alleluia.

PSALM XVIII. 18
For the end: a psalm of David.

THE heavens declare the glory of God, and the firmament proclaimeth the work of His hands.

Day unto day poureth forth speech, and night unto night proclaimeth knowledge.

There are no tongues nor words in which their voices are not heard.

Their sound hath gone forth into all the earth, and their words unto the ends of the world.

In the sun hath He set His tabernacle; and He, like a bridegroom coming forth from his chamber, will rejoice like a giant to run his course.

From the outermost border of heaven is His going forth, and His goal is unto the outermost part of heaven, and there shall no man hide himself from His heat.

The law of the Lord is blameless, converting souls; the testimony of the Lord is trustworthy, bringing wisdom to infants.

The statutes of the Lord are upright, gladdening the heart; the commandment of the Lord is far-shining, enlightening the eyes.

The fear of the Lord is pure, enduring for ever and ever; the judgments of the Lord are true, altogether justified,

More to be desired than gold and much precious stone, and sweeter than honey and the honeycomb.

Yea, for Thy servant keepeth them; in keeping them there is much reward.

As for transgressions, who will understand them? From my secret sins cleanse me, and from those of others spare Thy servant.

If they have not dominion over me, then blameless shall I be, and I shall be cleansed from great sin.

And the sayings of my mouth shall be unto Thy good pleasure, and the meditation of my heart shall be before Thee for ever, O Lord, my helper and redeemer.

PSALM XIX. 19

For the end: a psalm of David.

THE Lord hear thee in the day of affliction; the Name of the God of Jacob defend thee.

Let Him send forth unto thee help from His sanctuary, and out of Sion let Him help thee.

Let Him remember every sacrifice of thine, and thy whole-burnt offering let Him fatten.

The Lord grant thee according to thy heart, and fulfil all thy purposes.

We will rejoice in Thy salvation, and in the Name of the Lord our God shall we be magnified. The Lord fulfil all thy requests.

Now have I known that the Lord hath saved His anointed one; He will hearken unto him out of His holy heaven; in mighty deeds is the salvation of His right hand.

Some trust in chariots, and some in horses, but we will call upon the Name of the Lord our God.

They have been fettered and have fallen, but we are risen and are set upright.

O Lord, save the king, and hearken unto us in the day when we call upon Thee.

PSALM XX. 20

For the end: a psalm of David.

O LORD, in Thy strength the king shall be glad, and in Thy salvation shall he rejoice exceedingly.

The desire of his heart hast Thou granted unto him, and hast not denied him the requests of his lips.

Thou wentest before him with the blessings of goodness, Thou hast set upon his head a crown of precious stone.

He asked life of Thee, and Thou gavest him length of days unto ages of ages.

Great is his glory in Thy salvation; glory and majesty shalt Thou lay upon him.

For Thou shalt give him blessing for ever and ever, Thou shalt gladden him in joy with Thy countenance.

For the king hopeth in the Lord, and through the mercy of the Most High shall he not be shaken.

Let Thy hand be found on all Thine enemies; let Thy right hand find all that hate Thee.

For Thou wilt make them as an oven of fire in the time of Thy presence; the Lord in His wrath will trouble them sorely and fire shall devour them.

10 Their fruit wilt Thou destroy from the earth, and their seed from the sons of men.

For they have intended evil against Thee, they have devised counsels which they shall not be able to establish.

For Thou shalt make them turn their backs; among those that are Thy remnant, Thou shalt make ready their countenance.

Be Thou exalted, O Lord, in Thy strength; we will sing and chant of Thy mighty acts.

Glory. Both now. Alleluia.

PSALM XXI. 21

For the end: a psalm of David concerning help that cometh in the morning.

O GOD, my God, attend to me; why hast Thou forsaken me? Far from my salvation are the words of my transgressions.

My God, I will cry by day, and wilt Thou not hearken? and by night, and it shall not be unto folly for me.

But as for Thee, Thou dwellest in the sanctuary, O Praise of Israel.

In Thee have our fathers hoped; they hoped, and Thou didst deliver them.

5 Unto Thee they cried, and were saved; in Thee they hoped, and were not brought to shame.

But as for me, I am a worm, and not a man, a reproach of men, and the outcast of the people.

All that look upon me have laughed me to scorn; they have spoken with their lips and have wagged their heads:

He hoped in the Lord; let Him deliver him, let Him save him, for He desireth him.

For Thou art He that drewest me forth from the womb; my hope from the breasts of my mother.

On Thee was I cast from the womb; from my mother's womb, Thou art my God.

Depart not from me, for tribulation is nigh, for there is none to help me.

Many bullocks have encircled me, fat bulls have surrounded me.

They have opened their mouth against me, as might a lion ravenous and roaring.

I have been poured out like water, and scattered are all my bones; my heart is become like wax melting in the midst of my bowels.

My strength is dried up like a potsherd, and my tongue hath cleaved to my throat, and into the dust of death hast Thou brought me down.

For many dogs have encircled me, the congregation of evil-doers hath surrounded me; they have pierced my hands and my feet.

They have numbered all my bones, and they themselves have looked and stared upon me.

They have parted my garments amongst themselves, and for my vesture have they cast lots.

But Thou, O Lord, remove not Thy help far from me; attend unto mine aid.

Rescue my soul from the sword, even this only-begotten one of mine from the hand of the dog.

Save me from the mouth of the lion, and my lowliness from the horns of the unicorns.

I will declare Thy Name unto my brethren, in the midst of the church will I hymn Thee.

Ye that fear the Lord, praise Him; all ye that are of the seed of Jacob, glorify Him; let all fear Him that are of the seed of Israel.

For He hath not set at nought nor abhorred the supplications of the pauper, nor hath He turned His face from me; and when I cried unto Him, He hearkened unto me.

From Thee is my praise; in the great church will I confess Thee; my vows will I pay before them that fear Thee.

The poor shall eat and be filled, and they that seek the Lord shall praise Him; their hearts shall live for ever and ever.

All the ends of the earth shall remember and shall turn unto the Lord, and all the kindreds of the nations shall worship before Him.

For the kingdom is the Lord's and He Himself is sovereign of the nations.

All they that be fat upon the earth have eaten and worshipped; all they that go down into the earth shall fall down before Him.

Yea, my soul liveth for Him, and my seed shall serve Him.

The generation that cometh shall be told of the Lord, and they shall proclaim His righteousness to a people that shall be born, which the Lord hath made.

PSALM XXII. 22

A psalm of David.

The Lord is my shepherd, and I shall not want.

In a place of green pasture, there hath He made me to dwell; beside the water of rest hath He nurtured me.

He hath converted my soul, He hath led me on the paths of righteousness for His Name's sake.

For though I should walk in the midst of the shadow of death, I will fear no evil, for Thou art with me; Thy rod and Thy staff, they have comforted me.

5 Thou hast prepared a table before me in the presence of them that afflict me.

Thou hast anointed my head with oil, and Thy cup which filleth me, how excellent it is!

And Thy mercy shall pursue me all the days of my life, and I will dwell in the house of the Lord unto length of days.

PSALM XXIII. 23

A psalm of David, on the first day of the week.

The earth is the Lord's, and the fulness thereof, the world, and all that dwell therein.

He hath founded it upon the seas, and upon the rivers hath He prepared it.

Who shall ascend into the mountain of the Lord? Or who shall stand in His holy place?

He that is innocent in hands and pure in heart, who hath not received his soul in vain, and hath not sworn deceitfully to his neighbour.

5 Such a one shall receive a blessing from the Lord, and mercy from God his Saviour.

This is the generation of them that seek the Lord, of them that seek the face of the God of Jacob.

Lift up your gates, O ye princes; and be ye lifted up, ye everlasting gates, and the King of Glory shall enter in.

Who is this King of Glory? The Lord strong and mighty, the Lord, mighty in war.

Lift up your gates, O ye princes; and be ye lifted up, ye everlasting gates, and the King of Glory shall enter in.

10 Who is this King of Glory? The Lord of hosts, He is the King of Glory.

Glory. Both now. Alleluia.

THE FOURTH KATHISMA

PSALM XXIV. 24

A psalm of David.

UNTO Thee, O Lord, have I lifted up my soul.

O my God, in Thee have I trusted; let me never be put to shame, nor let mine enemies laugh me to scorn.

Yea, let none that wait on Thee be put to shame; let them be ashamed which are lawless without a cause.

Make Thy ways, O Lord, known unto me and teach me Thy paths.

Lead me in Thy truth and teach me, for Thou art God my Saviour; for on Thee have I waited all the day long.

Remember Thy compassions, O Lord, and Thy mercies, for they are from everlasting.

The sins of my youth and mine ignorances remember not; according to Thy mercy remember Thou me, for the sake of Thy goodness, O Lord.

Good and upright is the Lord; therefore will He set a law for them that sin in the way.

He will guide the meek in judgment, He will teach the meek His ways.

All the ways of the Lord are mercy and truth, unto them that seek after His covenant and His testimonies.

For the sake of Thy Name, O Lord, be gracious unto my sin; for it is great.

Who is the man that feareth the Lord? He will set him a law in the way which He hath chosen.

His soul shall dwell among good things, and his seed shall inherit the earth.

The Lord is the strength of them that fear Him, and His covenant shall be manifested unto them.

Mine eyes are ever toward the Lord, for He it is that will draw my feet out of the snare.

Look upon me, and have mercy on me; for I am one only-begotten and poor.

The afflictions of my heart are multiplied; bring me out from my necessities.

Behold my lowliness and my toil, and forgive all my sins.

Look upon mine enemies, for they are multiplied, and with an unjust hatred have they hated me.

Keep my soul and rescue me; let me not be put to shame, for I have hoped in Thee.

The innocent and the upright have cleaved unto me, for I waited on Thee, O Lord.

Redeem Israel, O God, out of all his afflictions.

PSALM XXV. 25

David's.

JUDGE me, O Lord, for in mine innocence have I walked; and hoping in the Lord I shall not grow weak.

Prove me, O Lord, and try me; prove with fire my reins and my heart.

For Thy mercy is before mine eyes, and I have been well-pleasing in Thy truth.

I have not sat with the council of vanity, nor shall I go in with them that transgress the law.

5 I have hated the congregation of evil-doers, and with the ungodly will I not sit.

I will wash my hands in innocency and I will compass Thine altar, O Lord, that I may hear the voice of Thy praise and tell of all Thy wondrous works.

O Lord, I have loved the beauty of Thy house, and the place where Thy glory dwelleth.

Destroy not my soul with the ungodly, nor my life with men of blood, in whose hands are iniquities; their right hand is full of bribes.

But as for me, in mine innocence have I walked; redeem me, O Lord, and have mercy on me.

10 My foot hath stood in uprightness; in the congregations will I bless Thee, O Lord.

PSALM XXVI. 26

David's. Before he was anointed.

THE Lord is my light and my saviour; whom then shall I fear? The Lord is the defender of my life; of whom then shall I be afraid?

When the wicked draw nigh against me to eat my flesh, they that afflict me and are mine enemies, they themselves became weak and they fell.

Though a host should array itself against me, my heart shall not be afraid; though war should rise up against me, in this have I hoped.

One thing have I asked of the Lord, this will I seek after: That I may dwell in the house of the Lord all the days

PSALM 26

of my life, that I may behold the delight of the Lord, and that I may visit His holy temple.

5 For He hid me in His tabernacle in the day of my troubles, He sheltered me in the secret place of His tabernacle, upon a rock hath He exalted me.

And now, behold, He exalted my head above mine enemies.

I went round about and I sacrificed in His tabernacle a sacrifice of praise and jubilation; I will sing and I will chant unto the Lord.

Hearken, O Lord, unto my voice, wherewith I cried; have mercy on me, and hearken unto me.

My heart said unto Thee: I will seek the Lord. My face hath sought after Thee; Thy face, O Lord, will I seek.

10 Turn not Thy face from me and turn not away in wrath from Thy servant.

Be Thou my helper; cast me not utterly away, and forsake me not, O God my Saviour.

For my father and my mother have forsaken me, but the Lord hath taken me to Himself.

Set me a law, O Lord, in Thy way, and lead me in the right path because of mine enemies.

Deliver me not over unto the souls of them that afflict me, for unjust witnesses are risen up against me, and injustice hath lied to itself.

15 I believe that I shall see the good things of the Lord in the land of the living.

Wait on the Lord; be thou manful, and let thy heart be strengthened, and wait on the Lord.

     Glory. Both now. Alleluia.

PSALM XXVII. 27
David's.

UNTO Thee, O Lord, will I cry; O my God, be not silent unto me, lest, if Thou be silent to me, I become like them that go down into the pit.

Hearken, O Lord, unto my supplication when I pray unto Thee, when I lift up my hands toward Thy holy temple.

Draw me not in with sinners, and with the workers of unrighteousness destroy me not, who speak peace with their neighbours, but evils are in their hearts.

Give unto them, O Lord, according to their deeds, and according to the wickedness of their endeavours; according to the work of their hands, give unto them. Render their reward unto them.

For they have not understood the works of the Lord, and the works of His hands. Thou shalt destroy them, and shalt not build them up.

Blessed is the Lord, because He hath heard the voice of my supplication.

The Lord is my helper and my defender; my heart hath hoped in Him, and I am helped and my flesh hath flourished again, and out of my desire will I confess Him.

The Lord is the strength of His people, and the champion of salvation for His anointed one.

Save Thy people and bless Thine inheritance; shepherd them and bear them up unto eternity.

PSALM XXVIII. 28

A psalm of David. A processional of the tabernacle.

BRING unto the Lord, ye sons of God, bring unto the Lord the sons of rams; bring unto the Lord glory and honour.

Bring unto the Lord the glory due unto His Name, worship the Lord in His holy court.

The voice of the Lord is upon the waters; the God of glory hath thundered, the Lord is upon the many waters.

The voice of the Lord in might, the voice of the Lord in majesty,

5 The voice of the Lord Who breaketh the cedars, yea, the Lord will break the cedars of Lebanon.

And He will break them small like the calf of Lebanon, and His beloved is like a son of the unicorns.

The voice of the Lord Who divideth the flame of fire,

The voice of the Lord Who shaketh the wilderness, yea, the Lord will shake the wilderness of Kaddis.

The voice of the Lord gathereth the harts, and shall reveal the thickets of oak, and in His temple every man uttereth glory.

10 The Lord dwelleth in the flood, yea, the Lord shall sit as king for ever.

The Lord will give strength unto His people; the Lord will bless His people with peace.

PSALM XXIX. 29

For the end: a canticle psalm at the dedication of the house of David.

I WILL exalt Thee, O Lord, for Thou hast upheld me, and hast not made my foes to rejoice over me.

O Lord my God, I cried unto Thee, and Thou hast healed me.

O Lord, Thou hast brought up my soul out of hades; Thou hast saved me from them that go down into the pit.

Chant unto the Lord, O ye saints of His, and give thanks at the remembrance of His holiness.

For wrath is in His anger, but in His will there is life; at evening shall weeping find lodging, but in the morning rejoicing.

And I said in my prosperity: I shall remain unshaken for ever.

O Lord, by Thy will hast Thou granted power to my beauty, but Thou hast turned away Thy face, and I am become troubled.

Unto Thee, O Lord, will I cry, and unto my God will I make supplication.

What profit is there in my blood when I go down into corruption? Shall dust confess Thee, or declare Thy truth?

The Lord hath heard me and hath had mercy on me; the Lord became my helper.

Thou hast turned my mourning into joy for me, Thou didst rend my sackcloth and didst gird me with gladness,

That my glory may chant unto Thee, and that I may not be pierced with sorrow; O Lord my God, I will confess Thee for ever.

Glory. Both now. Alleluia.

PSALM XXX. 30

For the end: a psalm of David, in time of sudden fear.

IN Thee, O Lord, have I hoped, let me not be put to shame in the age to come; in Thy righteousness deliver me, and rescue me.

Bow down Thine ear unto me, make haste to rescue me, be Thou unto me a God to defend me and a house of refuge to save me.

For my strength and my refuge art Thou, and for Thy Name's sake wilt Thou guide me and nourish me.

Thou wilt bring me out of this snare which they have hid for me, for Thou art my defender, O Lord.

5 Into Thy hands I will commit my spirit; Thou hast redeemed me, O Lord God of truth.

Thou hast hated them that cling to empty vanities; but I have hoped in the Lord.

I will rejoice and be glad in Thy mercy, for Thou hast regarded my lowliness; Thou hast saved my soul out of necessities,

And hast not shut me up in the hands of enemies; Thou hast set my feet in a spacious place.

Have mercy on me, O Lord, for I am afflicted; mine eye is troubled with anger, as also my soul and my belly.

10 For my life is spent with grief, and my years with groanings; my strength hath grown weak in poverty, and my bones are troubled.

I am become a reproach among all mine enemies, and greatly for my neighbours also, and a fear to mine acquaintances. They that saw me without fled from me.

I am forgotten by the heart like a dead man. I am become like a broken vessel.

For I have heard the reproach of many that dwell round about; when they assembled together against me, they devised to take away my life.

But as for me, I have hoped in Thee, O Lord; I said: Thou art my God; in Thy hands are my lots.

Deliver me from the hands of mine enemies, and from them that persecute me.

Make Thy face to shine upon Thy servant, save me in Thy mercy.

O Lord, let me not be put to shame, for I have called upon Thee; let the ungodly be put to shame and let them be brought down into hades.

Speechless be the deceitful lips which speak iniquity against the righteous man with arrogance and contempt.

How great is the multitude of Thy goodness, O Lord, which Thou hast hid for them that fear Thee, which Thou hast wrought for them that hope in Thee before the sons of men.

Thou shalt hide them in the secrecy of Thy presence from the disturbance of men; Thou shalt shelter them in the tabernacle from contradiction of tongues.

Blessed is the Lord, for He hath made His mercy wondrous in a fortified city.

But as for me, I said in mine ecstasy: I am cast away from the presence of Thine eyes. Therefore hast Thou heard the voice of my supplication when I cried unto Thee.

O love ye the Lord, all ye His saints, for the Lord requireth truth; and unto them that act with exceeding pride, He rendereth them their due.

Be ye manful, and let your heart be strengthened, all ye that hope in the Lord.

PSALM XXXI. 31

David's. Concerning instruction.

BLESSED are they whose iniquities are forgiven, and whose sins are covered.

Blessed is the man unto whom the Lord imputeth not sin, and in whose mouth there is no guile.

Because I kept silence, my bones are waxed old through my crying all the day long.

For day and night Thy hand was heavy upon me, I was reduced to misery whilst the thorn stuck fast in me.

Mine iniquity have I acknowledged, and my sin have I not hid. I said: I will confess mine iniquities before the Lord against myself. And Thou forgavest the ungodliness of my heart.

For this shall every one that is holy pray unto Thee in a seasonable time; moreover, in a flood of many waters shall they not come nigh unto him.

Thou art my refuge from the affliction which surroundeth me; O my Rejoicing, deliver me from them which have encircled me. (*Diapsalm*)

I will instruct thee and teach thee in this way which thou shalt go; I will fix Mine eyes upon thee.

Be ye not as the horse or as the mule which have no

understanding; whose jaws thou must hold with bit and bridle, lest they come nigh unto thee.

10 Many are the scourges of the sinner, but mercy shall encircle him that hopeth in the Lord.

Be glad in the Lord, and rejoice, ye righteous; and glory, all ye that are upright of heart.

> Glory. Both now. Alleluia.

THE FIFTH KATHISMA

PSALM XXXII. 32

David's. Without superscription among the Hebrews.

REJOICE in the Lord, O ye righteous; praise is meet for the upright.

Give praise to the Lord with the harp, chant unto Him with the ten-stringed psaltery.

Sing unto Him a new song, chant well unto Him with jubilation.

For the word of the Lord is true, and all His works are in faithfulness.

The Lord loveth mercy and judgment; the earth is full of the mercy of the Lord.

By the Word of the Lord were the heavens established, and all the might of them by the Spirit of His mouth,

Who gathereth together as into a wineskin the waters of the sea, Who layeth up the abysses in storehouses.

Let all the earth fear the Lord, and let all the inhabitants of the world be shaken before Him.

For He spake, and they came into being; He commanded, and they were created.

The Lord scattereth the plans of the heathens, He setteth aside the devices of the peoples, and He bringeth to nought the plans of princes.

But the counsel of the Lord abideth unto eternity, the thoughts of His heart unto generation and generation.

Blessed is the nation whose God is the Lord, the people whom He hath chosen for His inheritance.

The Lord looked down from heaven, He beheld all the sons of men.

From His habitation which He prepared, He looked upon all the inhabitants of the earth,

He that alone fashioned the heart of them, Who understandeth all their works.

A king is not saved by great might, nor shall a giant be saved by the magnitude of his own strength.

Futile is the horse for salvation, nor by the magnitude of his might shall he be saved.

Behold, the eyes of the Lord are upon them that fear Him, upon them that hope in His mercy.

To deliver their souls from death, and to nourish them in famine.

Our soul shall wait for the Lord, for He is our helper and our defender.

For our heart shall be glad in Him, and in His holy Name have we hoped.

Let Thy mercy, O Lord, be upon us, according as we have hoped in Thee.

PSALM XXXIII. 33

David's. When he changed his countenance before Abimelech, and was dismissed, and went away.

I WILL bless the Lord at all times, His praise shall continually be in my mouth.

In the Lord shall my soul be praised; let the meek hear and be glad.

O magnify the Lord with me, and let us exalt His Name together.

I sought the Lord, and He heard me, and delivered me from all my tribulations.

Come unto Him, and be enlightened, and your faces shall not be ashamed.

This poor man cried, and the Lord heard him, and saved him out of all his tribulations.

The angel of the Lord will encamp round about them that fear Him, and will deliver them.

O taste and see that the Lord is good; blessed is the man that hopeth in Him.

O fear the Lord, all ye His saints; for there is no want to them that fear Him.

Rich men have turned poor and gone hungry; but they that seek the Lord shall not be deprived of any good thing.

Come, ye children, hearken unto me; I will teach you the fear of the Lord.

What man is there that desireth life, who loveth to see good days?

Keep thy tongue from evil, and thy lips from speaking guile.

Turn away from evil, and do good; seek peace, and pursue it.

The eyes of the Lord are upon the righteous, and His ears are opened unto their supplication.

The face of the Lord is against them that do evil, utterly to destroy the remembrance of them from the earth.

The righteous cried, and the Lord heard them, and He delivered them out of all their tribulations.

The Lord is nigh unto them that are of a contrite heart, and He will save the humble of spirit.

Many are the tribulations of the righteous, and the Lord shall deliver them out of them all.

20 The Lord keepeth all their bones, not one of them shall be broken.

The death of sinners is evil, and they that hate the righteous shall do wrong.

The Lord will redeem the souls of His servants, and none of them will do wrong that hope in Him.

Glory. Both now. Alleluia.

PSALM XXXIV. 34
David's.

JUDGE them, O Lord, that do me injustice; war against them that war against me.

Take hold of weapon and shield, and arise unto my help.

Draw out a sword, and shut the way against them that persecute me; say to my soul: I am thy salvation.

Let them that seek my soul be shamed and confounded.

5 Let them be turned back, and be utterly put to shame, they that devise evils against me.

Let them become as dust before the face of the wind, an angel of the Lord also afflicting them.

Let their way become darkness and a sliding, an angel of the Lord also pursuing them.

For without cause have they secretly prepared for me destruction in their snare, without reason have they cast reproach on my soul.

Let a snare come upon him, which he knoweth not; and let the trap, which he hath hidden, catch him, and into that same snare let him fall.

10 But my soul shall rejoice in the Lord, it shall delight in His salvation.

All my bones shall say: Lord, O Lord, who is like unto Thee?

Delivering the beggar from the hand of them that are stronger than he, yea, poor man and pauper from them that despoil him.

Unjust witnesses rose up against me; things I knew not they asked me.

They repaid me with evil things for good, and barrenness for my soul.

15 But as for me, when they troubled me, I put on sackcloth.

And I humbled my soul with fasting, and my prayer shall return to my bosom.

As though it had been a neighbour, as though it had been our brother, so sought I to please; as one mourning and sad of countenance, so humbled I myself.

Yet against me they rejoiced and gathered together; scourges were gathered together upon me, and I knew it not.

They were rent asunder, yet not pricked at heart; they tempted me, they mocked me with mockery, they gnashed upon me with their teeth.

20 O Lord, when wilt Thou look upon me? Deliver my soul from their evil doing, even this only-begotten one of mine from the lions.

I will confess Thee in the great congregation; among a mighty people will I praise Thee.

Let not them rejoice against me that unjustly are mine

enemies, they that hate me without a cause, and wink with their eyes.

For peaceably indeed they spake unto me, but in their wrath were they devising deceits.

And they opened wide their mouth against me; they said: Well done, well done, our eyes have seen it.

25 Thou hast seen it, O Lord; keep not silence. O Lord, depart not from me.

Arise, O Lord, and be attentive unto my judgment, my God, and my Lord, unto my cause.

Judge me, O Lord, according to Thy righteousness; O Lord my God, let them not rejoice against me.

Let them not say in their hearts: Well done, well done, our soul. Let them not say: We have swallowed him up.

Let them be shamed and confounded together who rejoice at my woes.

30 Let them be clothed with shame and confusion who speak boastful words against me.

Let them rejoice and be glad who desire the righteousness of my cause, and let them that desire the peace of Thy servant say continually: The Lord be magnified.

And my tongue shall treat of Thy righteousness, and of Thy praise all the day long.

PSALM XXXV. 35

For the end: of David, the child of the Lord.

THE transgressor, that he may sin, saith to himself, that there is no fear of God before his eyes.

For he hath wrought craftiness before Him, lest he should find his iniquity and hate it.

The words of his mouth are iniquity and deceit, he hath not willed to understand how to do good.

Iniquity hath he devised upon his bed, he hath set himself in every way that is not good, and evil hath he not abhorred.

5 O Lord, Thy mercy is in heaven, and Thy truth reacheth unto the clouds.

Thy righteousness is as the mountains of God, Thy judgments are a great abyss.

Men and beasts wilt Thou save, O Lord. How Thou hast multiplied Thy mercy, O God!

Let the sons of men hope in the shelter of Thy wings.

They shall be drunken with the fatness of Thy house, and of the torrent of Thy delight shalt Thou make them to drink.

10 For in Thee is the fountain of life, in Thy light shall we see light.

O continue Thy mercy unto them that know Thee, and Thy righteousness unto the upright of heart.

Let not the foot of pride come against me, nor let the hand of a sinner move me.

Yonder be fallen all they that work iniquity; they are cast out, and shall not be able to stand.

Glory. Both now. Alleluia.

PSALM XXXVI. 36

David's.

Fret not thyself because of evil-doers, nor envy them that work iniquity.

For like grass quickly shall they be withered, and like green herbs quickly shall they fall away.

Hope in the Lord, and do good, and dwell on the earth, and like a shepherd shalt thou be fed with its riches.

Delight thyself in the Lord, and He will give thee the askings of thy heart.

Disclose unto the Lord thy way, and trust in Him, and He shall bring it to pass.

And He shall bring forth thy righteousness as the light and thy judgment as the noonday.

Submit thyself unto the Lord and supplicate Him; fret not thyself because of him that prospereth in his way, nor because of a man that doeth iniquity.

Cease from wrath and forsake anger; fret not thyself so as to do evil.

For evil-doers shall utterly perish, but they that wait on the Lord, they shall inherit the earth.

And yet a little while, and the sinner shall not be, and thou shalt seek for his place, and shalt not find it.

But the meek shall inherit the earth and shall delight themselves in an abundance of peace.

The sinner will diligently keep watch over the righteous man and will gnash with his teeth upon him.

But the Lord shall laugh at him, because He foreseeth that his day will come.

The sinners have drawn a sword; they have bent their bow, to cast down poor man and pauper, to slay the upright in heart.

Let their sword enter into their own hearts and let their bows be broken.

Better is the little which the just man hath than the great riches of sinners.

For the arms of the sinners shall be broken, but the Lord upholdeth the righteous.

The Lord knoweth the ways of the blameless and their inheritance shall be for ever.

They shall not be put to shame in an evil time, and in days of famine they shall be filled.

But the sinners shall perish, and the enemies of the Lord, in the moment when they are glorified and exalted, vanish away, and like smoke have vanished away.

The sinner borroweth and will not repay, but the just man showeth mercy and giveth.

For they that bless him shall inherit the earth, but they that curse him shall utterly perish.

By the Lord are the steps of a man rightly directed, and His way shall he greatly desire.

When he falleth he shall not be utterly cast down; for the Lord upholdeth his hand.

I have been young, and now indeed I am old, and I have not seen the righteous man forsaken, nor his seed begging bread.

All the day long the righteous showeth mercy, and lendeth, and his seed shall be unto blessing.

Decline from evil and do good, and dwell unto ages of ages.

For the Lord loveth judgment, and He will not forsake His holy ones; they shall be kept for ever.

But the wicked shall be banished, and the seed of the ungodly shall be utterly destroyed.

₃₀ The righteous shall inherit the earth and shall dwell therein unto ages of ages.

The mouth of the righteous shall meditate wisdom and his tongue shall speak of judgment.

The law of his God is in his heart, and his steps shall not be tripped.

The sinner watcheth the righteous one, and seeketh to slay him.

But the Lord will not abandon him to his hands, nor in any way condemn him when He judgeth him.

₃₅ Wait on the Lord and keep His way, and He shall exalt thee to inherit the earth; when sinners are utterly destroyed, thou shalt see it.

I have seen the ungodly man highly exalted and lifting himself up like the cedars of Lebanon.

But I passed by, and lo, he was not; and I sought him, and his place was not to be found.

Keep innocence, and behold uprightness, for there is a remnant for the peaceable man.

But the transgressors shall be utterly destroyed together, and the remnants of the ungodly shall be utterly destroyed.

₄₀ But the salvation of the righteous is from the Lord, and He is their defender in a time of affliction.

And the Lord shall help them and shall deliver them, and He will rescue them from sinners and will save them because they hoped in Him.

    Glory. Both now. Alleluia.

THE SIXTH KATHISMA

PSALM XXXVII. 37

A psalm of David. In remembrance, concerning the Sabbath.

O LORD, rebuke me not in Thine anger, nor chasten me in Thy wrath.

For Thine arrows are fastened in me, and Thou hast laid Thy hand heavily upon me.

There is no healing in my flesh in the face of Thy wrath; and there is no peace in my bones in the face of my sins.

For mine iniquities are risen higher than my head; as a heavy burden have they pressed heavily upon me.

My bruises are become noisome and corrupt in the face of my folly.

I have been wretched and utterly bowed down until the end; all the day long I went with downcast face.

For my loins are filled with mockings, and there is no healing in my flesh.

I am afflicted and humbled exceedingly, I have roared from the groaning of my heart.

O Lord, before Thee is all my desire, and my groaning is not hid from Thee.

My heart is troubled, my strength hath failed me; and the light of mine eyes, even this is not with me.

My friends and my neighbours drew nigh over against me and stood, and my nearest of kin stood afar off.

And they that sought after my soul used violence; and they that sought evils for me spake vain things, and craftinesses all the day long did they meditate.

But as for me, like a deaf man I heard them not, and was as a speechless man that openeth not his mouth.

And I became as a man that heareth not, and that hath in his mouth no reproofs.

For in Thee have I hoped, O Lord; Thou wilt hearken unto me, O Lord my God.

For I said: Let never mine enemies rejoice over me; yea, when my feet were shaken, those men spake boastful words against me.

For I am ready for scourges, and my sorrow is continually before me.

For I will declare mine iniquity, and I will take heed concerning my sin.

But mine enemies live and are made stronger than I, and they that hated me unjustly are multiplied.

They that render me evil for good slandered me, because I pursued goodness.

Forsake me not, O Lord my God, depart not from me.

Be attentive unto my help, O Lord of my salvation.

PSALM XXXVIII. 38

For the end: an ode of David for Idithum.

I SAID: I will take heed to my ways lest I sin with my tongue.

I set a guard for my mouth, when the sinner stood up against me.

I was dumb and was humbled, and held my peace, even from good, and my sorrow was stirred anew.

PSALM 38

My heart grew hot within me, and in my meditation a fire was kindled.

I spake with my tongue: O Lord, make me to know mine end, and the number of my days, what it is, that I may know what I lack.

Behold, Thou hast made my days as the spans of a hand, and my being is as nothing before Thee.

Nay, all things are vanity, every man living.

Surely man walketh about like a phantom, nay, in vain doth he disquiet himself.

He layeth up treasure, and knoweth not for whom he shall gather it.

And now, what is my patient endurance? Is it not the Lord? Yea, my hope is from Thee.

From all mine iniquities deliver me; Thou hast made me a reproach to the foolish.

I was dumb and opened not my mouth, for Thou hast made me.

Take away from me Thy scourges; for from the strength of Thy hand I have fainted.

With reprovings for iniquity hast Thou chastened man, and hast made his life to melt away like a spider's web; nay, in vain doth every man disquiet himself.

Hearken unto my prayer, O Lord, and unto my supplication; give ear unto my tears.

Be not silent, for I am a sojourner with Thee, and a stranger, as were all my fathers.

Spare me, that I may be refreshed before I go hence, and be no more.

PSALM XXXIX. 39

For the end: a psalm of David.

WITH patience I waited patiently for the Lord, and He was attentive unto me, and He hearkened unto my supplication.

And He brought me up out of the pit of misery, and from the mire of clay.

And He set my feet upon a rock, and He ordered my steps aright.

And He hath put into my mouth a new song, a hymn unto our God.

Many shall see, and shall fear, and shall hope in the Lord.

Blessed is the man, whose hope is in the Name of the Lord, and who hath not looked upon vanities and false frenzies.

Many, O Lord my God, are Thy wonders which Thou hast wrought, and in Thy thoughts there is none that shall be likened unto Thee.

I declared and spake: They are multiplied beyond number.

Sacrifice and offering hast Thou not desired, but a body hast Thou perfected for me.

Whole-burnt offerings and oblations for sin hast Thou not demanded.

Then I said: Behold, I am come (in the heading of the book it is written concerning me) to do Thy will, O my God, and Thy law is in the midst of my bowels.

I have proclaimed the good tidings of Thy righteousness in the great congregation; lo, my lips I shall not restrain; Lord, Thou knowest it.

Thy righteousness have I not hid in my heart; Thy truth and Thy salvation have I declared.

I have not concealed Thy mercy, nor Thy truth, from the great assemblage.

15 But Thou, O Lord, remove not Thy compassions far from me; let Thy mercy and Thy truth continually help me.

For evils without number have encompassed me; mine iniquities took hold of me, and I became unable to see.

They are multiplied more than the hairs of my head, and my heart hath failed me.

Be pleased, O Lord, to deliver me; O Lord, be attentive unto helping me.

Let them be shamed and confounded together which seek after my soul, to destroy it.

20 Let them be turned back and confounded that desire evils for me.

Let them quickly receive shame for their reward, who say to me: Well done, well done.

Let them rejoice and be glad in Thee all they that seek after Thee, O Lord; and let them that love Thy salvation continually say: The Lord be magnified.

But as for me, a poor man am I and a pauper; the Lord will care for me.

My helper and my defender art Thou, O my God; make no tarrying.

    Glory. Both now. Alleluia.

PSALM XL. 40

For the end: a psalm of David.

BLESSED is the man that hath understanding for the poor man and the pauper; in an evil day the Lord will deliver him.

May the Lord keep him, and make him to live, and make him blessed upon the earth, and never surrender him into the hands of his enemies.

May the Lord help him on his bed of pain, the whole of his confinement in his sickness hast Thou turned to the better.

I said: O Lord, have mercy on me, heal my soul, for I have sinned against Thee.

5 Mine enemies have spoken evil things against me: When shall he die, and when shall his name perish?

And though he came in to see me, his heart spake vanity; he gathered iniquity unto himself; he went forth, and spake in a like manner.

All mine enemies whispered against me, against me they devised evils for me.

An unjust word they set against me: Can it be that he that sleepeth shall rise up again?

Yea, even the man of my peace in whom I hoped, who ate of my bread, hath magnified the lifting of heels against me.

10 But Thou, O Lord, be merciful unto me, and raise me up, and I will requite them.

By this I know that Thou hast delighted in me, because mine enemy shall not rejoice over me.

And because of mine innocence Thou hast helped me, and hast established me before Thee for ever.

Blessed is the Lord God of Israel, from everlasting to everlasting. So be it. So be it.

PSALM XLI. 41

For the end: for instruction to the sons of Kore.

As the hart panteth after the fountains of water, so panteth my soul after Thee, O God.

My soul thirsted for God, the mighty, the living; when shall I come, and appear before the face of God?

My tears have been my bread by day and by night, whilst it is said to me daily: Where is thy God?

These things have I remembered, and I poured out my soul within me, for I shall go to the place of the wondrous tabernacle, even to the house of God, with a voice of rejoicing and thanksgiving, yea, of the sound of them that keep festival.

5 Why art thou cast down, O my soul? And why dost thou disquiet me?

Hope in God, for I will give thanks unto Him; He is the salvation of my countenance, and my God.

Within me my soul hath been troubled; therefore will I remember Thee from the land of Jordan and Hermonicm, from the little mountain.

Deep calleth unto deep, at the voice of Thy cataracts; all Thy billows and Thy waves have passed over me.

By day the Lord will command His mercy, and by night His ode shall be with me, my prayer unto the God of my life.

10 I will say unto God: Thou art my helper. Why hast Thou forgotten me? And wherefore go I with downcast face whilst mine enemy afflicteth me?

Whilst my bones were broken, mine enemies reproached me; whilst they said to me daily: Where is thy God?

Why art thou cast down, O my soul? And why dost thou disquiet me? Hope in God, for I will give thanks unto Him; He is the salvation of my countenance, and my God.

PSALM XLII. 42

For the end: a psalm of David, without superscription among the Hebrews.

Judge me, O God, and give judgment in my cause, against a nation that is not holy; from a man unjust and crafty deliver me.

For Thou, O God, art my strength. Wherefore hast Thou cast me off? And wherefore go I with downcast face whilst mine enemy afflicteth me?

O send out Thy light and Thy truth; they have guided me along the way, and have brought me unto Thy holy mountain, and unto Thy tabernacles.

And I shall go in unto the altar of God, unto God Who giveth gladness to my youth; I will give praise unto Thee, O God, my God, with the harp.

5 Why art thou cast down, O my soul? And why dost thou disquiet me? Hope in God, for I will give thanks unto Him; He is the salvation of my countenance, and my God.

Glory. Both now. Alleluia.

PSALM XLIII. 43

For the end: for instruction to the sons of Kore.

O GOD, with our ears have we heard, for our fathers have told us the work which Thou hadst wrought in their days, in the days of old.

Thy hand utterly destroyed the heathen, and in their stead Thou didst plant them; Thou didst bring evils upon those peoples, and didst cast them out.

For not by their own sword did they inherit the land, nor did their own arm save them,

But Thy right hand, and Thine arm, and the light of Thy countenance, because Thou wast well-pleased in them.

5 Thou Thyself art my King, and my God, Thou that commandest the salvation of Jacob.

Through Thee shall the horn of our strength push down our enemies, and through Thy Name shall we bring to nought them that rise up against us.

For not in my bow will I hope, and my sword shall not save me.

For Thou hast saved us from them that afflict us, and them that hate us hast Thou put to shame.

In God we will boast all the day long, and in Thy Name will we give praise in the age to come.

10 But now Thou hast cast us off and put us to shame, and wilt not go forth, O God, with our hosts.

Thou hast made us to turn back before our enemies, and they that hate us took spoils for themselves.

Thou hast given us up as sheep to be eaten, and among the nations hast Thou scattered us.

Thou hast sold Thy people without a price, and there was no gain in the selling of us.

Thou hast made us a reproach to our neighbours, a scorn and derision to them that are round about us.

15 Thou hast made us a byword among the nations, a shaking of head among the peoples.

All the day long my disgrace is before me, and the shame of my face hath covered me,

Because of the voice of him that reproacheth and revileth, because of the face of the enemy and pursuer.

All this hath come upon us, and we have not forgotten Thee, nor have we dealt unrighteously in Thy covenant.

Though our heart hath not turned back, yet Thou hast turned aside our paths from Thy ways.

20 For Thou hast humbled us in a place of affliction, and the shadow of death hath covered us.

If we have forgotten the Name of our God, and if we have stretched out our hands to a strange god,

Shall not God search out these things? For He knoweth the secrets of the heart.

For Thy sake we are slain all the day long, we are counted as sheep for the slaughter.

Rise up, why sleepest Thou, O Lord? Arise, and cast us not off at the end.

25 Wherefore turnest Thou Thy face away? Dost Thou forget our poverty and our affliction?

For our soul hath been humbled down to the dust, our belly hath cleaved to the earth.

Arise, O Lord, help us, and redeem us for Thy Name's sake.

PSALM XLIV. 44

For the end: concerning those verses that are to be alternated, for instruction to the sons of Kore. An ode concerning the Beloved One.

My heart hath poured forth a good word; I speak of my works to the king; my tongue is the pen of a swiftly writing scribe.

Comely art Thou in beauty more than the sons of men; grace hath been poured forth on Thy lips, wherefore God hath blessed Thee for ever.

Gird Thy sword upon Thy thigh, O Mighty One, in Thy comeliness and Thy beauty. And bend Thy bow, and proceed prosperously, and be king, because of truth and meekness and righteousness; and Thy right hand shall guide Thee wondrously.

Thine arrows are sharp, O Mighty One, (under Thee shall peoples fall) sharp in the heart of the enemies of the king.

5 Thy throne, O God, is for ever and ever; a sceptre of uprightness is the sceptre of Thy kingdom.

Thou hast loved righteousness and hated iniquity. Wherefore God, Thy God, hath anointed Thee with the oil of gladness more than Thy fellows.

Myrrh and stacte and cassia exhale from Thy garments, from the ivory palaces, whereby they have made Thee glad, they the daughters of kings in Thine honour.

At Thy right hand stood the queen, arrayed in a vesture of inwoven gold, adorned in varied colours.

Hearken, O daughter, and see, and incline thine ear; and forget thine own people and thy father's house.

And the King shall greatly desire thy beauty, for He Himself is thy Lord, and thou shalt worship Him.

And Him shall the daughters of Tyre worship with gifts; the rich among the people shall entreat thy countenance.

All the glory of the daughter of the King is within, with gold-fringed garments is she arrayed, adorned in varied colours.

The virgins that follow after her shall be brought unto the King, those near her shall be brought unto Thee.

They shall be brought with gladness and rejoicing, they shall be brought into the temple of the King.

In the stead of thy fathers, sons are born to thee; thou shalt make them princes over all the earth.

I shall commemorate thy name in every generation and generation.

Therefore shall peoples give praise unto thee for ever, and unto the ages of ages.

PSALM XLV. 45

For the end: a psalm of David, concerning hidden things, for the sons of Kore.

Our God is refuge and strength, a helper in afflictions which mightily befall us.

Therefore shall we not fear when the earth be shaken, nor when the mountains be removed into the heart of the seas.

Their waters roared and were troubled, the mountains were troubled by His might.

The rushings of the river make glad the city of God; the Most High hath hallowed His tabernacle.

God is in the midst of her, she shall not be shaken; God shall help her right early in the morning.

The nations were troubled, kingdoms tottered, the Most High gave forth His voice, the earth was shaken.

The Lord of hosts is with us, our helper is the God of Jacob.

Come and behold the works of God, what marvels He hath wrought on the earth, making wars to cease unto the ends of the earth.

He will crush the bow and will shatter the weapon, and shields will He utterly burn with fire.

Be still, and know that I am God; I will be exalted among the nations, I will be exalted in the earth.

The Lord of hosts is with us, our helper is the God of Jacob.

Glory. Both now. Alleluia.

THE SEVENTH KATHISMA

PSALM XLVI. 46

For the end: a psalm concerning the sons of Kore.

CLAP your hands, all ye nations; shout unto God with a voice of rejoicing,

For the Lord Most High is terrible, a great King over all the earth.

He hath subdued peoples under us, and nations under our feet.

He hath chosen us for His inheritance, the beauty of Jacob, which He loved.

5 God is gone up in jubilation, the Lord with the voice of the trumpet.

O chant unto our God, chant ye; chant unto our King, chant ye.

For God is king of all the earth, O chant ye with understanding.

God is king over the nations, God sitteth upon His holy throne.

The princes of the peoples are gathered together with the God of Abraham; for God's mighty ones of the earth are greatly exalted.

PSALM XLVII. 47

An ode for the sons of Kore, for the second day of the week.

GREAT is the Lord, and greatly to be praised, in the city of our God, in His holy mountain, in the well-rooted joy of all the earth,

The mountains of Sion on the sides of the north, the city of the great King.

God is known in her towers, when He cometh to help her.

For lo, the kings of the earth were assembled; they came together.

5 When they saw her thus they marvelled, they were troubled, they were shaken, trembling took hold of them; there were pangs as of a woman in travail.

With a vehement wind shalt Thou shatter the ships of Tharsis.

Even as we have heard, so too we have seen in the city of the Lord of hosts, in the city of our God. God hath laid her foundations unto eternity.

We have thought, O God, of Thy mercy in the midst of Thy people.

According to Thy Name, O God, so is Thy praise also unto the ends of the earth; Thy right hand is full of righteousness.

10 Let Mount Sion be glad, and let the daughters of Judea rejoice, because of Thy judgments, O Lord.

Encircle Sion and encompass her; tell her story in her towers.

Set your hearts upon her strength, and consider her bulwarks, that ye may tell it to another generation.

For He is our God for ever, yea, for ever and ever; He shall shepherd us unto the ages.

PSALM XLVIII. 48

For the end: a psalm for the sons of Kore.

HEAR this, all ye nations; give ear, all ye that inhabit the world,

Both ye that are born of earth, and ye sons of men, rich and poor men together.

My mouth shall speak wisdom, and the meditation of my heart shall be of understanding.

I will incline mine ear unto a parable, I will unfold my problem on the psaltery.

5 Wherefore should I fear in an evil day? The iniquity at my heel shall compass me about.

There be some that trust in their strength, and boast themselves in the multitude of their riches.

A brother cannot redeem; shall a man redeem?

He shall not give to God a ransom for himself, nor the price of the redemption of his own soul, though he hath laboured for ever, and shall live to the end.

For he shall not see corruption, when he shall see wise men dying.

10 The mindless man and the witless shall perish together, and they shall leave their riches to others.

And their graves shall be their houses unto eternity, their dwelling places unto generation and generation, though they have called their lands after their own names.

And man, being in honour, did not understand; he is compared to the mindless cattle, and is become like unto them.

This way of theirs is a stumbling-block for them, yet afterwards they will please with their mouth.

Like sheep they are laid in hades, death shall be their shepherd.

And the upright shall have dominion over them in the morning, and their help shall wax old in hades; they have been cast out from their glory.

Yet God shall redeem my soul out of the hand of hades, when he receiveth me.

Be not afraid when a man becometh rich, nor when the glory of his house is increased.

For when he dieth he shall carry nothing away, nor shall his glory descend after him.

For his soul shall be blessed in his lifetime; he will acknowledge Thee while Thou doest good unto him.

He shall enter into the generation of his fathers; he shall not see light unto eternity.

And man, being in honour, did not understand; he is compared to the mindless cattle, and is become like unto them.

Glory. Both now. Alleluia.

PSALM XLIX. 49

A psalm of Asaph.

THE God of gods, the Lord, hath spoken, and He hath called the earth from the rising of the sun and unto the setting thereof.

Out of Sion is the magnificence of His comeliness.

God shall come visibly, yea, our God, and shall not keep silence.

Fire shall blaze before Him, and round about Him shall there be a mighty tempest.

He shall summon heaven above and the earth that He may judge His people.

Gather together unto Him His holy ones who have established His covenant upon sacrifices.

And the heavens shall declare His righteousness, for God is judge.

Hear, O my people, and I will speak unto thee, O Israel, and I will testify against thee; I am God, thy God.

Not for sacrifices will I reprove thee; nay, thy whole-burnt offerings are continually before Me.

I will not welcome bullocks out of thy house, nor he-goats out of thy flocks.

For Mine are all the beasts of the field, cattle on the mountains, and oxen.

I know all the fowls of the air, and with Me is the beauty of the field.

If I hunger, not to thee will I tell it; for Mine is the world, and the fulness thereof.

Shall I eat of the flesh of bulls? Or the blood of goats, shall I drink it?

Sacrifice unto God a sacrifice of praise, and pay unto the Most High thy vows.

And call upon Me in the day of thine affliction, and I will deliver thee, and thou shalt glorify Me.

But unto the sinner God hath said: Why declarest thou My statutes and takest up My covenant in thy mouth?

Thou hast hated instruction, and hast cast out My words behind thee.

If thou sawest a thief, thou didst run with him; and with the adulterer thou hast set thy portion.

20 Thy mouth hath abounded with evil, and thy tongue hath woven deceits.

Thou didst sit down and speak against thy brother, and against thine own mother's son didst thou lay a stumbling-block; these things thou didst, and I kept silence.

Thou didst think an iniquity, that I should be like unto thee; I will reprove thee, and bring thy sins before thy face.

Wherefore, understand these things, ye that forget God, lest He snatch you away and there be none to deliver you.

A sacrifice of praise shall glorify Me, and there is the way wherein I shall show unto him My salvation.

PSALM L. 50

For the end: a psalm of David, when Nathan the Prophet came unto him, when he went in unto Bersabee, the wife of Urias.

HAVE mercy on me, O God, according to Thy great mercy; and according to the multitude of Thy compassions blot out my transgression.

Wash me thoroughly from mine iniquity, and cleanse me from my sin.

For I know mine iniquity, and my sin is ever before me.

Against Thee only have I sinned and done this evil before Thee, that Thou mightest be justified in Thy words, and prevail when Thou art judged.

5 For behold, I was conceived in iniquities, and in sins did my mother bear me.

For behold, Thou hast loved truth; the hidden and secret things of Thy wisdom hast Thou made manifest unto me.

Thou shalt sprinkle me with hyssop, and I shall be made clean; Thou shalt wash me, and I shall be made whiter than snow.

Thou shalt make me to hear joy and gladness; the bones that be humbled, they shall rejoice.

Turn Thy face away from my sins, and blot out all mine iniquities.

10 Create in me a clean heart, O God, and renew a right spirit within me.

Cast me not away from Thy presence, and take not Thy Holy Spirit from me.

Restore unto me the joy of Thy salvation, and with Thy governing Spirit establish me.

I shall teach transgressors Thy ways, and the ungodly shall turn back unto Thee.

Deliver me from blood-guiltiness, O God, Thou God of my salvation; my tongue shall rejoice in Thy righteousness.

15 O Lord, Thou shalt open my lips, and my mouth shall declare Thy praise.

For if Thou hadst desired sacrifice, I had given it; with whole-burnt offerings Thou shalt not be pleased.

A sacrifice unto God is a broken spirit; a heart that is broken and humbled God will not despise.

Do good, O Lord, in Thy good pleasure unto Sion, and let the walls of Jerusalem be builded.

Then shalt Thou be pleased with a sacrifice of righteousness, with oblation and whole-burnt offerings.

20 Then shall they offer bullocks upon Thine altar.

Glory. Both now. Alleluia.

PSALM LI. 51

For the end: concerning instruction by David, when
Doek the Idumean came, and declared to Saul, and said unto him:
David is come to the house of Abimelech.

WHY dost thou boast in evil, O mighty man, and in iniquity all the day long?

Thy tongue hath devised unrighteousness, like a sharpened razor hast thou wrought deceit.

Thou hast loved evil more than goodness, unrighteousness more than to speak righteousness.

Thou hast loved all the words of engulfing ruin, and a deceitful tongue.

5 Wherefore, God will destroy thee at the end, He will pluck thee out and remove thee from thy dwelling place, and thy root out of the land of the living.

The righteous shall see and fear, and shall laugh at him, and say:

Lo, this is the man that made not God his helper, but trusted in the abundance of his riches, and strengthened himself in his vanity.

But as for me, I am like a fruitful olive tree in the house of the Lord; I have hoped in the mercy of God for ever, and unto the ages of ages.

I will give praise unto Thee for ever, for what Thou

hast done, and I will wait on Thy Name, for it is good before Thy saints.

PSALM LII. 52

For the end: concerning Maeleth. Concerning instruction by David.

THE fool hath said in his heart: There is no God. They are corrupt and are abominable in iniquities; there is none that doeth good.

God looked down from heaven upon the sons of man, to see if there be any that understand or seek after God.

They are all gone astray, they are altogether rendered useless; there is none that doeth good, no not one.

5 Shall not all they that work iniquity come to understanding, they that eat up my people as they eat bread?

They have not called upon the Lord. There have they feared with fear where no fear is.

For God hath scattered the bones of man-pleasers; they have been put to shame, because God hath set them at nought.

Who shall give out of Sion the salvation of Israel? When God hath turned back the captivity of His people, Jacob shall rejoice and Israel shall be glad.

PSALM LIII. 53

For the end: among the hymns of instruction
by David, when the Ziphites came, and said to Saul:
Lo, is not David hidden with us?

O GOD, in Thy Name save me, and in Thy strength do Thou judge me.

O God, hearken unto my prayer, give ear unto the words of my mouth.

For strangers are risen up against me, and mighty men have sought after my soul and have not set God before themselves.

For behold, God helpeth me, and the Lord is the protector of my soul.

He will bring evils upon mine enemies. Utterly destroy them by Thy truth.

Willingly shall I sacrifice unto Thee; I will confess Thy Name, O Lord, for it is good.

For out of every affliction hast Thou delivered me, and mine eye hath looked down upon mine enemies.

PSALM LIV. 54

For the end: among the hymns of instruction by David.

GIVE ear, O God, unto my prayer, and disdain not my supplication; attend unto me, and hear me.

I was grieved in my meditation, and I was troubled at the voice of the enemy and at the oppression of the sinner;

Because they have turned iniquity upon me, and with wrath were they angry against me.

My heart is troubled within me, and the terror of death is fallen upon me.

Fear and trembling are come upon me, and darkness hath covered me.

And I said: Who will give me wings like a dove? And I will fly, and be at rest.

Lo, I have fled afar off and have dwelt in the wilderness.

I waited for God that saveth me from faint-heartedness and from tempest.

Plunge them into the depths, O Lord, and divide their tongues, for I have seen iniquity and gainsaying in the city.

Day and night they go round about her upon her walls; iniquity and toil and unrighteousness are in the midst of her.

And usury and deceit have not departed from her streets.

For if mine enemy had reviled me, I might have endured it.

And if he that hateth me had spoken boastful words against me, I might have hid myself from him.

But thou it was, O man of like soul with me, my guide and my familiar friend,

Thou who together with me didst sweeten my repasts; in the house of God I walked with thee in oneness of mind.

Let death come upon such ones, and let them go down alive into hades.

For wickedness is in their dwellings, and in the midst of them.

As for me, unto God have I cried, and the Lord hearkened unto me.

Evening, morning, and noonday will I tell of it and will declare it, and He will hear my voice.

He will redeem my soul in peace from them that draw nigh unto me, for they among many were with me.

God will hear, and He will humble them, He that is before the ages.

For to them there is no requital, because they have not feared God; He hath stretched forth His hand in retribution.

They have defiled His covenant; they were scattered by the wrath of His countenance, and their hearts have convened.

Their words were smoother than oil, and yet they are darts.

Cast thy care upon the Lord, and He will nourish thee; He will never permit the righteous to be shaken.

But Thou, O God, shalt bring those men down into the pit of destruction.

Bloody and deceitful men shall not live out half their days; but as for me, O Lord, I will hope in Thee.

Glory. Both now. Alleluia.

THE EIGHTH KATHISMA

PSALM LV. 55

For the end: concerning the people distant from the Holies. By David, for a pillar inscription, when the foreigners took him in Geth.

Have mercy on me, O God, for man hath trodden me down all the day long; making war, he hath afflicted me.

Mine enemies have trodden me down all the day long, for many are they that war against me from on high. By day I shall not fear; but as for me, I will hope in Thee.

In God will I commend my words, in God I have set my hope; I will not fear what flesh shall do to me.

All the day long they detested my words, all their thoughts were against me for evil.

They will dwell near and will hide themselves; they will watch where I set my heel, even as they have waited for my soul.

On no account wilt Thou save them, in wrath wilt Thou bring down the peoples, O God.

My life have I declared unto Thee; Thou hast set my tears before Thee.

Even as in Thy promise, mine enemies shall be turned back.

In what day soever I shall call upon Thee, behold, I know that Thou art God.

In God will I praise His word, in the Lord will I praise His speech; in God have I put my hope, I will not fear what man shall do unto me.

In me, O God, there be vows, which I will render in praise of Thee.

For Thou hast delivered my soul from death, mine eyes from tears, and my feet from sliding, that I may be well-pleasing before the Lord in the light of the living.

PSALM LVI. 56

For the end: destroy not. By David; for a pillar inscription, when he fled from the presence of Saul to the cave.

HAVE mercy on me, O God, have mercy on me, for my soul trusted in Thee.

And in the shadow of Thy wings will I hope, until iniquity shall pass away.

I will cry unto God the Most High, unto God my benefactor.

He hath sent out of heaven and saved me, He hath given over to reproach them that were trampling me down.

God hath sent forth His mercy and His truth, and hath delivered my soul from the midst of lions' cubs; I laid me down to sleep as one troubled.

As for the sons of men, their teeth are weapons and arrows, and their tongue a sharp sword.

Be Thou exalted above the heavens, O God, and Thy glory above all the earth.

They have prepared a snare for my feet, and bowed down my soul.

They have dug a pit before my face and have fallen into it themselves.

Ready is my heart, O God, ready is my heart; I will sing and chant in my glory.

Awake, O my glory; awake, O psaltery and harp; I myself will awake at dawn.

I will confess Thee among the peoples, O Lord, I will chant unto Thee among the nations.

For magnified even unto the heavens is Thy mercy, and Thy truth even unto the clouds.

Be Thou exalted above the heavens, O God, and Thy glory above all the earth.

PSALM LVII. 57

For the end: destroy not. By David; for a pillar inscription.

IF ye indeed speak of righteousness, judge rightly, ye sons of men.

For in your heart ye work iniquity in the earth; your hands weave unrighteousness.

Even from the womb, sinners are estranged; even from the belly, they are gone astray, they have spoken lies.

Their rage is like that of a serpent, like that of an asp that is deaf and stoppeth her ears,

Which shall not hearken to the voice of the charmers, nor is spellbound by the spells of a wizard.

God will shatter their teeth in their mouth, the great teeth of the lions the Lord hath broken.

They shall vanish like passing waters; He will bend His bow till they be weakened.

Like wax that is melted shall they be taken away; fire hath fallen upon them and they saw not the sun.

Before your thorns can know their brier, while they are yet alive, in His wrath shall He swallow them up.

10 The righteous man shall be glad, when he seeth the avengement, he shall wash his hands in the blood of the sinner.

And man shall say: If indeed there is fruit for the righteous man, there is indeed a God that judgeth them upon the earth.

Glory. Both now. Alleluia.

PSALM LVIII. 58

For the end: destroy not. By David; for a pillar inscription, when Saul sent and watched his house to slay him.

Rescue me from mine enemies, O God, and from them that rise up against me redeem me.

Deliver me from them that work iniquity, and from men of blood do Thou save me.

For lo, they have hunted after my soul, the mighty have set upon me.

Neither is it mine iniquity, O Lord, nor my sin; without iniquity I ran, and directed my steps; arise to meet me, and behold.

5 And Thou, O Lord God of hosts, the God of Israel, be attentive to visit all the heathen; be not merciful to any that work iniquity.

They shall return at evening, and shall hunger like dogs, and shall go round about the city.

Behold, they shall utter sounds with their mouth, and a sword is in their lips: For who, say they, hath heard?

And Thou, O Lord, shalt laugh them to scorn; Thou shalt bring to nought all the heathen.

O my Strength, I will keep watch for Thee, for Thou, O God, art my helper.

10 As for my God, His mercy shall go before me; my God shall make it manifest unto me among mine enemies.

Slay them not, lest at any time they forget Thy law; scatter them by Thy power, and bring them down, O Lord my defender.

The sin of their mouth is the speech of their lips; yea, let them be taken captive in their pride.

And from their curse and falsehood shall their final destruction be made known in the wrath of their utter destruction, and they shall be no more.

And they shall know that God is sovereign of Jacob and of the ends of the earth.

15 They shall return at evening, and shall hunger like dogs, and shall go round about the city.

They shall be scattered abroad that they may eat; if they be not satisfied, they shall murmur.

But as for me, I will sing of Thy power; and in the morning I will rejoice in Thy mercy.

For Thou art become my helper and my refuge in the day of my tribulation.

Thou art my helper, unto Thee will I chant; for Thou, O God, art my helper; O my God, Thou art my mercy.

PSALM LIX. 59

For the end: concerning those verses that are to be alternated; furthermore, for the pillar inscription of David, for instruction when he had burned Mesopotamia of Syria and Syrian Sobal, and Joab had returned and had smitten Edom, even twelve thousand in the Valley of Salt.

O GOD, Thou hast cast us off and hast destroyed us; Thou hast been wroth and hast had pity upon us.

Thou madest the earth to quake and didst trouble it; heal the breaches thereof, for it hath been shaken.

Thou hast shown Thy people hard things, Thou hast made us to drink the wine of contrition.

Thou hast given a sign unto them that fear Thee, that they may flee from before the face of the bow.

That Thy beloved ones may be delivered, save Thou with Thy right hand and hearken unto me.

God hath spoken in His sanctuary: I will rejoice and I will divide Sikima, and the vale of tabernacles will I measure out.

Mine is Galaad, and Mine is Manasses, and Ephraim is the strength of My head.

Judah is My king, Moab is the cauldron of My hope.

Upon Idumea will I stretch out My shoe; the foreign tribes have been subjected unto Me.

Who will bring me into a fortified city? Or who will lead me into Idumea?

Wilt Thou not, O God, Who hast spurned us? And wilt Thou not, O God, go forth with our forces?

Give us help from affliction, for vain is the salvation of man.

In God we shall work mighty deeds, and He will bring to nought them that afflict us.

PSALM LX. 60

For the end: among the hymns of David.

Hearken, O God, unto my supplication; attend unto my prayer.

From the ends of the earth unto Thee have I cried, when my heart was despondent; on a rock hast Thou lifted me on high.

Thou hast guided me, for Thou art become my hope, a tower of strength against the face of the enemy.

I will dwell in Thy tabernacle unto the ages, I shall be sheltered in the shelter of Thy wings.

5 For Thou, O God, hast heard my prayers; Thou hast given an inheritance to them that fear Thy Name.

Days shalt Thou add to the days of the king, his years unto days for generation and generation.

He shall abide before the face of God in the age to come. As for His mercy and truth, who shall seek them out?

So will I chant unto Thy Name unto the ages, that I may pay my vows from day to day.

Glory. Both now. Alleluia.

PSALM LXI. 61

For the end: a psalm of David concerning Idithum.

Shall not my soul be subjected to God? For from Him is my salvation.

For He is my God, my saviour and my helper, and I shall be shaken no more.

How long do ye assail a man? Ye kill, all of you, as ye might assail a leaning wall and a tottering rampart.

But they made plans to cast aside mine honour, they ran in falsehood; with their mouth they bless, but with their heart they curse.

5 But be subject unto God, O my soul, for from Him is my patient endurance.

For He is my God, my saviour and my helper, and I shall not be moved from hence.

In God is my salvation and my glory; He is the God of my help, and my hope is in God.

Hope in Him, all ye congregation of the peoples; pour out your hearts before Him, for God is our helper.

For the sons of men are vain, the sons of men are a lie in the balance; out of vanity they gather themselves together that they might do injustice.

10 Set not your hopes on injustice, and lust not after plunder; if riches flow in, set not your hearts thereon.

Once hath God spoken; these two things have I heard, that dominion belongeth to God, and mercy is Thine, O Lord; for Thou wilt render to every man according to his works.

PSALM LXII. 62

A psalm of David, when he was in the wilderness of Judea.

O GOD, my God, unto Thee I rise early at dawn. My soul hath thirsted for Thee; how often hath my flesh longed after Thee in a land barren and untrodden and unwatered.

So in the sanctuary have I appeared before Thee to see Thy power and Thy glory,

For Thy mercy is better than lives; my lips shall praise Thee.

So shall I bless Thee in my life, and in Thy Name will I lift up my hands.

5 As with marrow and fatness let my soul be filled, and with lips of rejoicing shall my mouth praise Thee.

If I remembered Thee on my bed, at the dawn I meditated on Thee.

For Thou art become my helper; in the shelter of Thy wings will I rejoice.

My soul hath cleaved after Thee, Thy right hand hath been quick to help me.

But as for these, in vain have they sought after my soul; they shall go into the nethermost parts of the earth, they shall be surrendered unto the edge of the sword; portions for foxes shall they be.

10 But the king shall be glad in God, everyone shall be praised that sweareth by Him; for the mouth of them is stopped that speak unjust things.

PSALM LXIII. 63

For the end: a psalm of David.

HEARKEN, O God, unto my prayer, when I make supplication unto Thee; rescue my soul from fear of the enemy.

Shelter me from the concourse of them that do wickedness, from the multitude of them that work unrighteousness.

They have sharpened their tongues like a sword, they have bent their bow, a bitter thing, that they may shoot in secret at the blameless man.

Suddenly shall they shoot at him and shall not fear; they have strengthened themselves in a wicked word.

5 They have spoken of hiding snares; they said: Who shall see them?

They have searched after iniquity, in searching they are grown weary of searching.

A man shall draw nigh, and the heart is deep; and God shall be exalted.

As an arrow of infants are their blows, and their tongues are made strengthless against them.

All that saw them were troubled, and every man was afraid.

10 And they declared the works of God, and His deeds they understood.

The righteous man shall be glad in the Lord, and shall hope in Him; and all the upright in heart shall be praised.

Glory. Both now. Alleluia.

THE NINTH KATHISMA

PSALM LXIV. 64

For the end: a canticle psalm of David, an ode sung by Jeremias and Ezekiel and the captive people when they were about to depart.

To Thee is due praise, O God, in Sion; and unto Thee shall a vow be rendered in Jerusalem.

Hearken unto my prayer, for unto Thee shall all flesh come.

The words of lawless men have overpowered us, but to our ungodliness shalt Thou be merciful.

Blessed is he whom Thou hast chosen and hast taken to Thyself; he shall dwell in Thy courts.

We shall be filled with the good things of Thy house; holy is Thy temple, wonderful in righteousness.

Hearken unto us, O God our Saviour, Thou hope of all the ends of the earth and of them that be far off at sea,

Who settest fast the mountains by Thy strength, Who art girded round about with power, Who troublest the hollow of the sea; as for the roar of its waves, who shall withstand them?

The heathen shall be troubled, and the dwellers of the farthest regions shall be afraid at Thy signs; Thou shalt make the outgoings of the morning and the evening to delight.

Thou hast visited the earth and abundantly watered her; Thou hast multiplied the means of enriching her.

The river of God is filled with waters; Thou hast prepared their food, for thus is the preparation thereof.

Do Thou make her furrows drunk with water, multiply her fruits; in her showers will she be glad when she sprouteth forth.

Thou shalt bless the crown of the year with Thy goodness, and Thy plains shall be filled with fatness.

Enriched shall be the mountains of the wilderness, and the hills shall be girded with rejoicing.

The rams of the flock have clothed themselves with fleece, and the valleys shall abound with wheat; they shall cry aloud, yea, they shall chant hymns unto Thee.

PSALM LXV. 65

For the end: a psalmic ode of resurrection.

SHOUT with jubilation unto the Lord, all the earth; chant ye unto His Name, give glory in praise of Him.

Say unto God: How awesome are Thy works! In the multitude of Thy power shall Thine enemies be proved false unto Thee.

Let all the earth worship Thee and chant unto Thee; let them chant unto Thy Name, O Most High.

Come and see the works of the Lord, how awesome He is in His counsels, more than the sons of men.

He turneth the sea into dry land; in the river shall they pass through on foot.

There shall we rejoice in Him, in Him that is ruler in His sovereignty for ever.

His eyes look upon the nations; let not them that embitter Him be exalted in themselves.

O bless our God, ye nations, and make the voice of His praise to be heard,

Who hath established my soul in life, and permitteth not my feet to be shaken.

10 For Thou hast proved us, O God, and by fire hast Thou tried us even as silver is tried by fire.

Thou hast brought us into the snare, Thou hast laid afflictions upon our back, Thou madest men to mount upon our heads.

We went through fire and water, and Thou didst bring us out into refreshment.

I will go into Thy house with a whole-burnt offering; to Thee will I pay my vows which my lips pronounced and which my mouth had spoken in mine affliction.

Whole-burnt offerings full of marrow will I offer unto Thee, with incense and rams; oxen and goats will I offer unto Thee.

15 Come and hear, and I will declare unto you, all ye that fear God, what things He hath done for my soul.

Unto Him with my mouth have I cried, and I exalted Him with my tongue.

If in my heart I regarded unrighteousness, let the Lord not hear me.

Wherefore God hath hearkened unto me, He hath been attentive to the voice of my supplication.

Blessed is God Who hath not turned away my prayer, nor His mercy away from me.

PSALM LXVI. 66

For the end: among the hymns. A canticle psalm of David.

GOD be gracious unto us and bless us, and cause His face to shine upon us and have mercy on us,

That we may know upon the earth Thy way, among all the nations Thy salvation.

Let the peoples give Thee praise, O God, let all the peoples praise Thee.

Let the nations be glad and rejoice, for Thou shalt judge peoples with uprightness; and nations shalt Thou guide upon the earth.

Let the peoples give Thee praise, O God, let all the peoples praise Thee; the earth hath yielded her fruit.

Let God, our God, bless us; let God bless us, and let all the ends of the earth fear Him.

Glory. Both now. Alleluia.

PSALM LXVII. 67

For the end: a canticle psalm of David.

LET God arise and let His enemies be scattered, and let them that hate Him flee from before His face.

As smoke vanisheth, so let them vanish; as wax melteth before the fire, so let sinners perish at the presence of God.

And let the righteous be glad; let them rejoice in the presence of God, let them delight in gladness.

Sing unto God, chant unto His Name; prepare ye the way for Him that rideth upon the setting of the sun. Lord is His Name; yea, rejoice before Him.

Let them be troubled at His presence, Who is a father of orphans and a judge to the widows.

God is in His holy place, God settleth the solitary in a house,

Mightily leading forth them that were shackled, and likewise them that embitter Him, them that dwell in tombs.

O God, when Thou wentest forth before Thy people, when Thou didst traverse the wilderness,

The earth was shaken and the heavens dropped dew, at the presence of the God of Sinai, at the presence of the God of Israel.

A rain freely given shalt Thou ordain, O God, for Thine inheritance; yea, it became weak, but Thou shalt restore it.

Thy living creatures shall dwell therein; Thou hast prepared it in Thy goodness for the poor man, O God.

The Lord shall give speech with great power to them that bring good tidings.

He that is the King of the hosts of His beloved one shall divide the spoils for the beauty of the house.

Even if ye sleep among the lots, ye shall have the wings of a dove covered with silver, and her pinions of sparkling gold.

When He that is in the heavens ordaineth kings over her, they shall be made snow-white in Selmon.

The mountain of God is a butter mountain, a curdled mountain, a butter mountain.

Why suppose ye that there be other curdled mountains? This is the mountain wherein God is pleased to dwell, yea, for the Lord will dwell therein to the end.

The chariot host of God is ten thousandfold, yea, thousands of them that abound in number; the Lord is among them at Sinai, in His holy place.

Thou hast ascended on high, Thou leddest captivity captive, Thou didst receive gifts among men (yea, for they were disobedient) that Thou mightest dwell there.

20 Blessed is the Lord God, blessed is the Lord day by day; the God of our salvation shall prosper us along the way.

Our God is the God of salvation, and the pathways leading forth from death are those of the Lord's Lord.

But God shall crush the heads of His enemies, the hairy crown of them that continue in their trespasses.

The Lord said: I will return from Basan. I will return in the deeps of the sea,

That thy foot may be dipped in blood, yea, the tongue of thy dogs in that of thine enemies.

25 Thy processionals have been seen, O God, the processionals of my God, of my King Who is in His sanctuary.

Princes went before, and after them the chanters, in the midst of timbrel-playing maidens.

In congregations bless ye God, the Lord from the wellsprings of Israel.

Yonder is Benjamin the younger in rapture, the princes of Judah their rulers, the princes of Zabulon, the princes of Nephthalim.

Give Thou command, O God, unto Thy hosts; strengthen, O God, this which Thou hast wrought in us.

30 Because of Thy temple in Jerusalem, kings shall bring gifts unto Thee.

Rebuke the wild beasts of the reed, that congregation of bulls among the heifers of the peoples, lest they exclude them that have been proved like silver.

Scatter the nations that desire wars; ambassadors shall come out of Egypt; Ethiopia shall hasten to stretch out her hand unto God.

Ye kingdoms of the earth, sing unto God; chant ye unto the Lord, unto Him that rideth the heaven of heaven towards the dayspring. Lo, He will utter with His voice a voice of power.

Give ye glory unto God; His magnificence is over Israel and His power is in the clouds.

Wondrous is God in His saints; the God of Israel, He will give power and strength unto His people. Blessed is God.

Glory. Both now. Alleluia.

PSALM LXVIII. 68

For the end: concerning those verses that are to be alternated.
A psalm of David.

SAVE me, O God, for the waters are come in unto my soul.

I am stuck fast in the mire of the deep, and there is no sure standing.

I am come into the deeps of the sea, and a tempest hath overwhelmed me.

I am grown weary with crying, my throat is become hoarse; from my hoping in my God, mine eyes have failed me.

They that hate me without a cause are multiplied more than the hairs of my head.

PSALM 68

Mine enemies are grown strong, they that persecute me unjustly; then did I restore that which I took not away.

O God, Thou knowest my foolishness, and my transgressions are not hid from Thee.

Let not them that wait on Thee be ashamed for my sake, O Lord, Thou Lord of hosts.

Nor let them that seek after Thee be confounded for my sake, O God of Israel.

10 Because for Thy sake I have borne reproach, shame hath covered my face.

I am become a stranger unto my brethren, and an alien unto the sons of my mother.

For the zeal of Thy house hath eaten me up, and the reproaches of them that reproach Thee are fallen on me.

Yea, with fasting I covered my soul, and it was turned into a reproach for me.

And I made sackcloth my clothing, and I became a proverb to them.

15 And they prated against me, they that sit in the gates; and they made a song about me, they that drink wine.

But as for me, with my prayer I cry unto Thee, O Lord; it is time for Thy good pleasure.

O God, in the multitude of Thy mercy hearken unto me, in the truth of Thy salvation.

Save me from the mire, that I be not stuck therein; let me be delivered from them that hate me and from the deeps of the waters.

Let not the tempest of water overwhelm me, nor let the deep swallow me up, nor let the pit shut its mouth upon me.

Hearken unto me, O Lord, for Thy mercy is good; according to the multitude of Thy compassions, look upon me.

Turn not Thy countenance away from Thy servant, for I am afflicted; quickly hearken unto me.

Attend unto my soul and deliver it; because of mine enemies, rescue me.

For Thou knowest my reproach, my shame, and my humiliation.

Before Thee are all that afflict me; my soul hath awaited reproach and misery.

And I waited for one that would grieve with me, but there was no one; and for them that would comfort me, but I found none.

And they gave me gall for my food, and for my thirst they gave me vinegar to drink.

Let their table before them be for a snare, for a recompense and for a stumbling-block.

Let their eyes be darkened that they may not see, and their back do Thou continually bow down.

Pour out upon them Thy wrath, and let the fury of Thy wrath take hold upon them.

Let their habitation be made desolate, and in their tents let there be none to dwell.

For they persecuted him whom Thou hast smitten, and to the pain of my wounds have they added.

Add iniquity to their iniquity, and let them not enter into Thy righteousness.

Let them be blotted out of the book of the living, and with the righteous let them not be written.

Poor and in sorrow am I; may Thy salvation, O God, be quick to help me.

35 I will praise the Name of my God with an ode, I will magnify Him with praise.

And this shall please God more than a young calf that hath horns and hooves.

Let beggars behold it and be glad; seek after God, and your soul shall live.

For the Lord hath hearkened unto the poor and hath not despised them that are fettered for His sake.

Let the heavens and the earth praise Him, the sea and all the creeping things therein.

40 For God will save Sion, and the cities of Judea shall be builded; and they shall dwell therein and inherit it.

And the seed of Thy servants shall possess it, and they that love Thy Name shall dwell therein.

PSALM LXIX. 69

For the end: David's. In remembrance, that the Lord may save me.

O GOD, be attentive unto helping me; O Lord, make haste to help me.

Let them be shamed and confounded that seek after my soul.

Let them be turned back and brought to shame that desire evils against me.

Let them be turned back straightway in shame that say unto me: Well done! Well done!

5 Let them be glad and rejoice in Thee all that seek after Thee, O God, and let them that love Thy salvation say continually: The Lord be magnified.

But as for me, I am poor and needy; O God, come unto mine aid.

My helper and my deliverer art Thou, O Lord; make no long tarrying.

Glory. Both now. Alleluia.

THE TENTH KATHISMA

PSALM LXX. 70

David's. A psalm of the sons of Jonadab and the first that were taken away captive. Without superscription among the Hebrews.

In Thee, O Lord, have I hoped, let me not be put to shame in the age to come; in Thy righteousness deliver me and rescue me; incline Thine ear unto me and save me.

Be Thou unto me a God that is my defender and a place of strength that Thou mayest save me, for Thou art my foundation and refuge.

O my God, deliver me out of the hand of the sinner, out of the hand of the transgressor and the unrighteous man.

For Thou art my patience, O Lord; O Lord, Thou art my hope from my youth.

On Thee have I been made fast from the womb; from my mother's womb Thou art my protector.

In Thee continually is my singing of praise; I am become as a wonder to many, and Thou art my strong helper.

Let my mouth be filled with praise, that I may hymn Thy glory and Thy majesty all the day long.

Cast me not away in the time of mine old age; when my strength faileth, forsake me not.

For mine enemies have spoken against me, and they that watch my soul took counsel together, saying: God hath forsaken him; pursue him and take him for there is none to deliver him.

My God, be not far off from me; my God, be attentive unto helping me.

Let them be put to shame and brought to nought that falsely accuse my soul; let them be covered with shame and confusion, they that seek evils for me.

But as for me, I will ever hope in Thee, and I will add to all Thy praise.

My mouth shall declare Thy righteousness, all the day long Thy salvation; for I know not the reckoning thereof.

I will commence in the might of the Lord; O Lord, I will make mention of the righteousness which is Thine alone.

O my God, Thou hast taught me from my youth, and till now will I declare Thy wondrous works.

Yea, even unto old age and the dignity of years, my God, forsake me not,

Until I declare Thy mighty arm to every generation that is to come,

Yea, Thy sovereignty and Thy righteousness, O God, and declare even to the heights the great things which Thou hast done for me. O God, who is like unto Thee?

How great are the many and evil afflictions which Thou hast showed unto me; yet, having returned, Thou madest me to live, and out of the depths of the earth Thou broughtest me up.

Thou hast multiplied Thy magnificence over me; and having returned, Thou hast comforted me, and out of the depths of the earth again Thou broughtest me up.

Therefore also will I confess Thee among the peoples, O Lord, with instruments of psalmody; with the harp I will chant of Thy truth unto Thee, O God, O Holy One of Israel.

My lips shall rejoice when I chant unto Thee, yea, even my soul which Thou hast redeemed.

Moreover my tongue will meditate on Thy righteousness all the day long, when they be put to shame and confounded which seek evils for me.

PSALM LXXI. 71

For the end: a psalm of David, for Solomon.

O GOD, give Thy judgment to the king, and Thy righteousness to the son of the king,

That he may judge Thy people with righteousness, and Thy poor with judgment.

Let the mountains receive peace for the people, and let the hills receive righteousness.

He shall judge the beggars among the people, and shall save the sons of the poor, and shall humble the false accuser.

And He shall continue as long as the sun, and before the moon from generation to generation.

He shall come down like rain upon a fleece, and like rain-drops that fall upon the earth.

In His days shall rightcousness dawn forth an abundance of peace, until the moon be taken away.

And He shall have dominion from sea to sea, and from the rivers even unto the ends of the inhabited earth.

Before Him shall the Ethiopians fall down, and His enemies shall lick the dust.

The kings of Tharsis and the islands shall bring gifts, kings of the Arabians and of Saba shall bring presents.

And all the kings of the earth shall worship Him, all the nations shall serve Him,

For He hath delivered the beggar from the oppressor, and the poor man for whom there was no helper.

He shall spare the poor man and the pauper, and the souls of the poor shall He save.

From usury and from injustices shall He redeem their souls, and precious shall be His Name before them.

15 And He shall live, and there shall be given unto Him of the gold of Arabia, and they shall make prayer concerning Him always; all the day long shall they bless Him.

He shall be a support in the earth on the summits of the mountains; exalted more than Lebanon shall be His fruit, and they of the city shall flourish like the grass of the earth.

His Name shall be blessed unto the ages, before the sun doth His Name continue.

And in Him shall be blessed all the tribes of the earth, all the nations shall call Him blessed.

Blessed is the Lord, the God of Israel, Who alone doeth wonders.

20 And blessed is the Name of His glory for ever, and unto the ages of ages.

And all the earth shall be filled with His glory. So be it. So be it.

Glory. Both now. Alleluia.

The Hymns of David, the Son of Jesse, are ended.

PSALM LXXII. 72

A psalm for Asaph; an ode to the Assyrian.

How good is God to Israel, to them that are upright of heart!

But as for me, my feet were all but shaken; my steps well nigh had slipped.

For I was jealous of the transgressors, when I beheld the peace of sinners.

For they make no sign of refusal in the time of their death, and they have steadfastness in the time of their scourging.

5 They are not in such toils as other men, nor with other men shall they be scourged.

Wherefore, their pride hath utterly mastered them, they have wrapped themselves in their injustice and ungodliness.

Their injustice shall go forth as out of fatness, they have passed through to their heart's intent.

They have thought and spoken in wickedness, they have spoken unrighteousness in arrogance.

They have set their mouth against heaven, and their tongue roveth in the earth.

10 Therefore shall my people return hither, and full days shall be found in them.

And they said: How doth God know? And is there knowledge in the Most High?

Behold, these are the sinners; they prosper in this age and have obtained riches.

And I said: Surely in vain have I kept justice in my heart and washed my hands among the innocent.

And I became a man scourged all the day long, and reproof was mine in every morning.

15 And I said: I shall speak thus: Lo, I should have broken covenant with the generation of Thy sons.

And I sought to understand, but this was toilsome in my sight, until I come into the sanctuary of God and understand their end.

Surely, for their crafty dealings Thou hast appointed evils for them; Thou hast cast them down in their exaltation.

How are they come unto desolation in a moment! They have ceased to be; they have perished because of their iniquity.

As a dream of one who awaketh, O Lord, in Thy city Thou shalt bring their image to nought.

20 For my heart was fired and my reins have been changed; and I was brought to nought and knew it not.

I became as a beast before Thee, and I am ever with Thee.

Thou hast held me by my right hand, and by Thy counsel Thou hast guided me, and with glory hast Thou taken me to Thyself.

For what have I in heaven? And besides Thee, what have I desired upon earth?

My heart and my flesh have failed, O God of my heart; and God is my portion for ever.

25 For behold, they that remove themselves from Thee shall perish; Thou hast destroyed all that go a whoring from Thee.

But it is good for me to cleave unto God, to put my

hope in the Lord, that I may declare all Thy praises in the gates of the daughter of Sion.

PSALM LXXIII. 73
Asaph's. Concerning instruction.

O GOD, why hast Thou cast us off unto the end? Why hath Thine anger raged against the sheep of Thy pasture?

Remember Thy congregation which Thou hast purchased from the beginning.

Thou hast redeemed the rod of Thine inheritance, this Mount Sion wherein Thou hast dwelt.

Lift up Thy hands against their pride at the end, against the things which the enemy hath wickedly done in Thy holy place.

5 And they that hate Thee have boasted in the midst of Thy feast.

They set up their ensigns, yea, signs (though they knew it not) as it were for the departing on high.

As in a forest of trees, with axes they cut down the doors thereof together, with two-edged axe and mason's hammer have they broken it down.

With fire have they burned down Thy sanctuary, they have profaned even unto the ground the habitation of Thy Name.

They said in their heart, even the whole kindred of them together: Come, let us abolish all the feasts of God from the earth.

10 Our signs have we not seen; there is no more any prophet, and he will know us no more.

How long, O God, shall the enemy utter reproaches? Shall the adversary provoke Thy Name to the end?

Wherefore turnest away Thy hand, and Thy right hand out of the midst of Thy bosom for ever?

But God is our king before the ages, He hath wrought salvation in the midst of the earth.

Thou didst establish the sea by Thy might, Thou didst break the heads of the dragons in the water.

Thou didst crush the head of the dragon, Thou gavest him as food to the Ethiopian peoples.

Thou hast cloven fountains and torrents, Thou hast dried up the rivers of Etham.

Thine is the day and Thine is the night; Thou hast perfected the light and the sun.

Thou hast made all the borders of the earth; summer and spring hast Thou fashioned.

Be mindful of this Thy creation. The enemy hath reproached the Lord, and a mindless people hath provoked Thy Name.

O deliver not unto beasts the soul which doth confess Thee; of the souls of Thy paupers be not forgetful unto the end.

Look Thou upon Thy covenant, for the dark places of the earth are filled with the houses of iniquity.

Let not the humbled and shamed man be turned away; the beggar and the poor man shall praise Thy Name.

Arise, O God, judge Thine own cause; remember the reproach made against Thee by the mindless man all the day long.

Forget not the voice of Thy suppliants; the pride of them that hate Thee ascendeth continually.

Glory. Both now. Alleluia.

PSALM LXXIV. 74

For the end: destroy not. A canticle psalm for Asaph.

WE will confess Thee, O God, we will confess Thee, and we will call upon Thy Name.

I will tell of all Thy wonders. When I am given the appointed time, I will judge uprightly.

The earth is melted and all that dwell therein; it is I that made steadfast the pillars thereof.

I said to the transgressors: Do not transgress; and to the sinners: Lift not up the horn.

Lift not up your horn on high, and speak not unrighteousness against God.

For judgment cometh not from the byways, nor from the west, nor from the desert mountains; for God is judge.

This man He humbleth, and another He exalteth; for in the hand of the Lord there is a brimming cup of unmingled wine.

And He hath inclined it from side to side, but the dregs thereof were not fully emptied out; all the sinners of the earth shall drink of them.

But as for me, I will rejoice for ever; I will chant unto the God of Jacob.

And all the horns of the sinners will I break, but the horn of the righteous man shall be exalted.

PSALM LXXV. 75

For the end: among the hymns. A psalm for Asaph, an ode to the Assyrian.

IN Judea is God known, His Name is great in Israel.

And His place hath been made in peace, and His dwelling in Sion.

There did He break the power of the bow, the weapon and the sword and the battle.

Thou shinest wondrously from the everlasting mountains; all the foolish of heart were troubled.

5 They have slept their sleep, and all the men of wealth have found nothing in their hands.

At Thy rebuke, O God of Jacob, they that had mounted upon horses fell aslumber.

Thou art to be feared, and who shall withstand Thee? From thenceforth is Thy wrath; Thou didst cause judgment to be heard from heaven.

The earth feared and was still, when God rose to judgment to save all the meek of the earth.

For the inward thought of man shall give praise unto Thee, and the remainder of his inward thought shall keep a feast to Thee.

10 Make your vows and pay them to the Lord our God; all that are round about Him shall bring gifts,

To Him that is to be feared and taketh away the spirits of princes, to Him that is to be feared among the kings of the earth.

PSALM LXXVI. 76

For the end: a psalm for Asaph concerning Idithum.

WITH my voice unto the Lord have I cried, with my voice unto God, and He was attentive unto me.

In the day of mine affliction I sought out God, with my hands upraised by night before Him, and I was not deceived.

My soul refused to be comforted; I remembered God and I was gladdened; I spake in idleness and my spirit became faint-hearted.

Mine eyes were wakeful before the watches; I was troubled and spake not.

I thought upon the days of old, and the years of ages past I called to mind, and I meditated.

By night I pondered in my heart, and my spirit searched diligently.

Will the Lord then cast me off unto the ages, and will He be favourable no more?

Or will He cut off His mercy unto the end? Hath He brought to an end His word from generation to generation?

Or will the Lord forget to be merciful? Or in His wrath will He shut up His compassions for ever?

And I said: Now have I made a beginning; this change hath been wrought by the right hand of the Most High.

I remembered the works of the Lord; for I will remember Thy wonders from the beginning.

And I will meditate on all Thy works, and I shall ponder upon Thy ways.

O God, in the sanctuary is Thy way. What God is as great as our God? Thou art God Who workest wonders.

Thou hast made Thy power known among the peoples; with Thine arm hast Thou redeemed Thy people, the sons of Jacob and Joseph.

The waters saw Thee, O God, the waters saw Thee and were afraid; the abysses were troubled.

Great was the resounding sound of the waters, the clouds gave forth a voice.

Yea, for Thine arrows passed abroad; the voice of Thy thunder is in their rolling.

And Thy lightnings have lightened the world; the earth was shaken and it trembled.

In the sea are Thy byways, and Thy paths in many waters; and Thy footsteps shall not be known.

Thou leddest Thy people as sheep by the hand of Moses and Aaron.

Glory. Both now. Alleluia.

THE ELEVENTH KATHISMA

PSALM LXXVII. 77

Concerning instruction. For Asaph.

GIVE heed, O my people, to my law; incline your ear unto the words of my mouth.

I will open my mouth in parables, I will utter dark sayings which have been from the beginning,

Even those things that we have heard and have known and which our fathers have told us.

They were not hid from their children in another generation.

They declared the praises of the Lord and His mighty acts and His wonders which He wrought.

And He raised up a testimony in Jacob and appointed a law in Israel,

Even those things He had commanded our fathers, to make the same known unto their children, that another generation might know,

Even the sons about to be born, that they in turn might arise and declare them unto their sons,

That they might set their hope in God, and not forget the works of God, but seek after His commandments,

That they might not be as their fathers, a generation perverse and provoking,

A generation that set not their heart aright, and which kept not their spirit steadfast with God.

The sons of Ephraim that bend and shoot with bows turned back in the day of battle.

They kept not the covenant of God, and in His law they were not fain to walk.

They forgot His benefits and His wonders that He had showed to them, even the wonders He had done in the sight of their fathers, in the land of Egypt, and in the plain of Tanis.

15 He divided the sea, and brought them through; He made the waters to stand as in a wineskin.

He guided them with a cloud by day, and all the night with a light of fire.

He divided the rock in the wilderness, and gave them to drink as in a great deep.

He led forth water out of the rock, and brought down waters like rivers.

And they added yet more sin against Him, they embittered the Most High in the waterless place.

20 And they made trial of God in their hearts, by asking food for their souls.

And they spake against God, and they said: Cannot God prepare a table in the wilderness?

Because He smote a rock, and waters streamed forth, and the torrents overflowed,

Cannot He give bread also, or prepare a table for His people?

Wherefore, the Lord heard and was stirred up, and a fire was kindled in Jacob, and wrath rose up against Israel,

25 Because they believed not in God, nor hoped in His salvation.

And He commanded the clouds from above, and opened the doors of heaven,

And rained manna on them to eat, and bread of heaven did He give unto them.

Man ate the bread of angels; provision He sent them to the full.

He removed the south wind from heaven, and brought in by His might the southwest wind.

And He rained on them flesh as it were dust, and feathered birds like the sands of the sea,

Which fell in the midst of their camp, round about their tents.

And they ate and were filled exceedingly, and their desire did He give unto them; nor were they deprived of their desire.

But while their food was yet in their mouth, the wrath of God rose up against them.

And He slew their stout ones, and shackled the choice men of Israel.

In all these things they sinned the more, and believed not in His wonders.

And their days were consumed in vanity, and their years with haste.

When He slew them, then they sought after Him, and they turned back and enquired early after God.

And they remembered that God is their helper, and that God the Most High is their redeemer.

And they loved Him with their mouth, and with their tongue they lied to Him,

40 For their heart was not right with Him, nor were they faithful in His covenant.

But He is compassionate and will be gracious unto their sins, and He will not destroy.

And many a time will He turn His anger away, and will not kindle all His wrath.

And He remembered that they are but flesh, breath which passeth away and cometh not back again.

How often did they embitter Him in the wilderness, and move Him to wrath in the waterless land!

45 They turned back and made trial of God and provoked the Holy One of Israel.

They remembered not His hand, nor the day wherein He redeemed them from the hand of the oppressor,

How He had wrought in Egypt His signs, and His marvels in the plain of Tanis.

Yea, He had turned into blood their rivers and their rainfalls, that they might not drink.

He had sent against them the dog-fly, and it devoured them; and the frog, and it destroyed them.

50 And He had given to the cankerworm their fruits, and their labours to the locust.

And He destroyed with hail their vine, and their mulberry trees with frost.

And He had given over to the hail their cattle, and their substance to the fire.

And He sent forth against them the wrath of His anger, anger and wrath and affliction, a mission performed by evil angels.

He had made a path for His wrath, and He spared not

from death their souls, and their cattle He shut up in death.

⁵⁵ And He had smitten every firstborn in the land of Egypt, the firstlings of all their labour, in the tabernacles of Ham.

And He took away His people as sheep, and He led them forth as a flock in the wilderness.

And He guided them in hope and they feared not, and the sea covered up their enemies.

And He brought them unto the mountain of His sanctuary, this mountain which His right hand had gained as a possession.

He cast out the heathen from before their face, and apportioned them an inheritance by lot.

⁶⁰ And He settled in their tents the tribes of Israel.

But they tempted and embittered God the Most High, and His testimonies they did not keep.

And they turned back and brake covenant, even as their fathers did; they became like unto a crooked bow.

And they provoked Him to wrath among their hills, and with their graven images they moved Him to jealousy.

God heard and regarded them no more, and set Israel utterly at nought.

⁶⁵ And He rejected His dwelling at Silom, His dwelling where He had dwelt among men.

And He gave over to captivity their strength, and their beauty into the hands of enemies.

And with a sword He enclosed His people, and His inheritance did He regard no more.

Fire consumed their young men, and their virgins lamented not.

Their priests fell by the sword, and none shall weep for their widows.

70 And the Lord awoke as one that sleepeth, like a mighty man grown cloyed with wine.

And He smote His enemies upon their backs, reproach everlasting He gave to them.

And He rejected the dwelling of Joseph, and He chose not the tribe of Ephraim.

And He chose the tribe of Judah, Mount Sion which He loved.

And He built His sanctuary like that of a unicorn, on the earth He established it for ever.

75 And He chose out David His servant, and took him up from the flocks of sheep, from following the ewes great with young He took him,

To shepherd Jacob His servant, and Israel His inheritance.

And he did shepherd them in the innocence of his heart, and by the skilfulness of his hands he guided them.

Glory. Both now. Alleluia.

PSALM LXXVIII. 78

A psalm for Asaph.

O GOD, the heathen are come into Thine inheritance, they have defiled Thy holy temple; they have made Jerusalem as it were the hut of an orchard-keeper.

They have made the dead bodies of Thy servants to be

food for the birds of heaven, the flesh of Thy saints for the beasts of the earth.

They have poured out their blood like water round about Jerusalem, and there was none to bury them.

We are become a reproach among our neighbours, a scorn and derision to them that are round about us.

5 How long, O Lord, wilt Thou be wroth unto the end? Shall Thy jealousy be kindled like fire?

Pour out Thy wrath upon the nations that know Thee not, and upon the kingdoms that have not called upon Thy Name;

For they have devoured Jacob, and his place have they made desolate.

O remember not our iniquities of old; let Thy compassions quickly go before us, O Lord, for we are become exceedingly poor.

Help us, O God our Saviour, for the sake of the glory of Thy Name; O Lord, deliver us and be gracious unto our sins for Thy Name's sake,

10 Lest haply the nations say: Where is their God?

Yea, make known among the nations before our eyes the vengeance for Thy servants' blood which hath been shed. Let there come before Thee the groaning of them that be in fetters.

According to the greatness of Thine arm, show Thy care for the sons of the slain.

And render to our neighbours sevenfold into their bosom their reproach, wherewith they have reproached Thee, O Lord;

For we are Thy people and the sheep of Thy pasture. We will confess Thee, O God, for ever; unto generation and generation we will declare Thy praise.

PSALM LXXIX. 79

For the end: concerning those verses that are to be alternated.
A testimony for Asaph; a psalm concerning the Assyrian.

O SHEPHERD of Israel, attend, Thou that leadest Joseph like a sheep.

Thou that sittest on the cherubim, manifest Thyself before Ephraim and Benjamin and Manasses.

Stir up Thy might and come to save us.

O God, make us to return and cause Thy face to shine, and we shall be saved.

5 O Lord God of hosts, how long wilt Thou be wroth against the prayer of Thy servants?

Wilt Thou feed us with the bread of tears, and wilt Thou give us for drink tears in measure?

Thou hast made us a gainsaying among our neighbours, and our enemies have scoffed at us.

O Lord of hosts, make us to return and cause Thy face to shine, and we shall be saved.

A vine hast Thou brought out of Egypt, Thou hast cast out the heathen and planted it.

10 Thou hast prepared the way before it, and Thou hast planted the roots thereof, and it filled the earth.

The shadows thereof covered the mountains, and the boughs thereof the cedars of God.

It stretched forth its shoots unto the sea, and its branches unto the rivers.

Why hast Thou broken down the hedge thereof, and all that pass along the way do pluck the fruit?

The boar of the forest hath laid it to waste, and the wild beast hath devoured it.

15 O God of hosts, return again; and look down from heaven and behold, and visit this vine,

And perfect that which Thy right hand hath planted, and look upon the son of man whom Thou madest strong for Thyself.

It is burned with fire and is dug up; at the rebuke of Thy face they shall perish.

Let Thy hand be upon the man of Thy right hand, and upon the son of man whom Thou madest strong for Thyself.

And we will not depart from Thee; Thou shalt quicken us, and we will call upon Thy Name.

20 O Lord God of hosts, make us to return and cause Thy face to shine, and we shall be saved.

PSALM LXXX. 80

For the end: a canticle psalm for Asaph concerning the wine-presses.

REJOICE in God our helper, shout with joy to the God of Jacob.

Take up a psalm, and bring the timbrel, the pleasant psaltery with the harp.

Sound the trumpet at the new moon, in the notable day of our feast.

For this is an ordinance for Israel and a judgment of the God of Jacob.

⁵ He ordained it for a testimony in Joseph when he went out from the land of Egypt; a tongue which he knew not did he hear.

He removed his back from burdens; his hands had slaved at the basket.

Thou didst call upon Me in affliction, and I delivered thee; I heard thee in the secret place of the tempest, I made trial of thee at the water of gainsaying.

Hear, O My people, and I will speak unto thee, O Israel, and I will testify unto thee; if thou hearest Me, there shall be in thee no new god, nor shalt thou worship an alien god,

For I am the Lord thy God Who led thee out of the land of Egypt. Open thy mouth wide, and I will fill it.

¹⁰ But My people heard not My voice, and Israel gave no heed unto Me.

And I let them go according to the ways of their hearts; they shall walk in their own ways.

If My people had heard Me, if Israel had walked in My ways,

Quickly would I have humbled their enemies, and upon their oppressors would I have laid My hand.

The enemies of the Lord have lied unto Him, but in that age their time shall come.

¹⁵ And He fed them with the fat of the wheat, and with honey out of the rock He satisfied them.

Glory. Both now. Alleluia.

PSALM LXXXI. 81

A psalm for Asaph.

GOD stood in the congregation of the gods, and in the midst He shall stand out among gods.

How long will ye judge unrighteously and accept the person of sinners?

Judge for the orphan and the poor man, do justice to the humble and the pauper.

Rescue the poor man and the needy, from the hand of the sinner deliver him.

5 They have not known, nor understood; they walk in darkness. Let all the foundations of the earth be shaken.

I said: Ye are gods, and all of you the sons of the Most High.

But like men ye die, and like one of the rulers do ye fall.

Arise, O God, judge the earth, for Thou shalt have an inheritance among all the nations.

PSALM LXXXII. 82

A psalmic ode for Asaph.

O GOD, who shall be likened unto Thee? Be Thou not silent, neither be still, O God.

For behold, Thine enemies have made a noise, and they that hate Thee have lifted up their heads.

Against Thy people have they taken wicked counsel, and have conspired against Thy saints.

They said: Come, let us utterly destroy them that they may be no more a nation, and let the name of Israel be remembered no more.

5 For they have conspired with oneness of mind together, against Thee have they made a covenant; even the tents of the Idumeans and the Ismaelites,

Moab and the Hagarenes, Gebal and Ammon and Amalek, and foreigners with them that dwell at Tyre.

Yea, for even Assur is come with them; they are become a help for the sons of Lot.

Do unto them as Thou didst unto Madiam and Sisara, as unto Jabin at the brook of Kisson.

They were utterly destroyed in Endor, they became as dung for the earth.

10 Make their princes like Oreb and Zeb and Zebee and Salmana.

Yea, all their princes who said: Let us take to ourselves for an inheritance the sanctuary of God.

O my God, make them like a wheel, as stubble before the face of the wind,

As fire which shall burn the forest, as a flame which shall consume the mountains.

So shalt Thou pursue them with Thy tempest, and in Thy wrath shalt Thou trouble them.

15 Fill their faces with dishonour, and they shall seek Thy Name, O Lord.

Let them be shamed and troubled unto ages of ages, and let them be confounded and destroyed.

And let them know that Thy Name is Lord; Thou alone art Most High over all the earth.

PSALM LXXXIII. 83

For the end: concerning the wine-presses; for the sons of Kore.

How beloved are Thy dwellings, O Lord of hosts; my soul longeth and fainteth for the courts of the Lord.

My heart and my flesh have rejoiced in the living God.

For the sparrow hath found herself a house, and the turtledove a nest for herself where she may lay her young,

Even Thine altars, O Lord of hosts, my King and my God.

5 Blessed are they that dwell in Thy house; unto ages of ages shall they praise Thee.

Blessed is the man whose help is from Thee; he hath made ascents in his heart, in the vale of weeping, in the place which he hath appointed.

Yea, for the lawgiver will give blessings; they shall go from strength to strength, the God of gods shall be seen in Sion.

O Lord of hosts, hearken unto my prayer; give ear, O God of Jacob.

O God, our defender, behold, and look upon the face of Thine anointed one.

10 For better is one day in Thy courts than thousands elsewhere.

I have chosen rather to be an outcast in the house of my God than to dwell in the tents of sinners.

For the Lord loveth mercy and truth, God will give grace and glory; the Lord will not withhold good things from them that walk in innocence.

O Lord God of hosts, blessed is the man that hopeth in Thee.

PSALM LXXXIV. 84

For the end: a psalm for the sons of Kore.

Thou hast been gracious, O Lord, unto Thy land; Thou hast turned back the captivity of Jacob.

Thou hast forgiven the iniquities of Thy people, Thou hast covered all their sins.

Thou hast made all Thy wrath to cease, Thou hast turned back from the wrath of Thine anger.

Turn us back, O God of our salvation, and turn away Thine anger from us.

5 Wilt Thou be wroth with us unto the ages? Or wilt Thou draw out Thy wrath from generation to generation?

O God, Thou wilt turn and quicken us, and Thy people shall be glad in Thee.

Show us, O Lord, Thy mercy, and Thy salvation do Thou give unto us.

I will hear what the Lord God will speak in me; for He will speak peace to His people and to His saints and to them that turn their heart unto Him.

Surely nigh unto them that fear Him is His salvation, that glory may dwell in our land.

10 Mercy and truth are met together, righteousness and peace have kissed each other.

Truth is sprung up out of the earth, and righteousness hath looked down from heaven.

Yea, for the Lord will give goodness, and our land shall yield her fruit.

Righteousness shall go before Him and shall set His footsteps in the way.

Glory. Both now. Alleluia.

THE TWELFTH KATHISMA

PSALM LXXXV. 85

A prayer of David.

Bow down Thine ear, O Lord, and hearken unto me, for poor and needy am I.

Preserve my soul, for I am holy; save Thy servant, O my God, that hopeth in Thee.

Have mercy on me, O Lord, for unto Thee will I cry all the day long; make glad the soul of Thy servant, for unto Thee have I lifted up my soul.

For Thou, O Lord, art good and gentle, and plenteous in mercy unto all them that call upon Thee.

Give ear, O Lord, unto my prayer, and attend unto the voice of my supplication.

In the day of mine affliction have I cried unto Thee, for Thou hast heard me.

There is none like unto Thee among the gods, O Lord, nor are there any works like unto Thy works.

All the nations whom Thou hast made shall come and shall worship before Thee, O Lord, and shall glorify Thy Name.

For Thou art great and workest wonders; Thou alone art God.

Guide me, O Lord, in Thy way, and I will walk in Thy truth; let my heart rejoice that I may fear Thy Name.

I will confess Thee, O Lord my God, with all my heart, and I will glorify Thy Name for ever.

For great is Thy mercy upon me, and Thou hast delivered my soul from the nethermost hades.

O God, transgressors have risen up against me, and the assembly of the mighty hath sought after my soul, and they have not set Thee before them.

But Thou, O Lord my God, art compassionate and merciful, long-suffering and plenteous in mercy, and true.

Look upon me and have mercy upon me; give Thy strength unto Thy servant, and save the son of Thy handmaiden.

Work in me a sign unto good, and let them that hate me behold and be put to shame; for Thou, O Lord, hast holpen me and comforted me.

PSALM LXXXVI. 86

A canticle psalm, for the sons of Kore.

His foundations are in the holy mountains; the Lord loveth the gates of Sion more than all the dwellings of Jacob.

Glorious things are spoken of thee, O city of God.

I will make mention of Raab and Babylon to them that know me.

And lo, the foreigners and Tyre and the people of the Ethiopians, these were born there.

A man will say: Mother Sion; and: That man was born in her; and: The Most High Himself hath founded her.

The Lord shall tell it in the writ of the peoples and the princes, even these that were born in her.

How joyous are all they that have their habitation in Thee.

PSALM LXXXVII. 87

A psalmic ode for the sons of Kore. For the end: concerning the response of Maeleth, concerning the giving of a wise instruction to Aemon the Israelite.

O LORD God of my salvation, by day have I cried and by night before Thee.

Let my prayer come before Thee, bow down Thine ear unto my supplication,

For filled with evils is my soul, and my life unto hades hath drawn nigh.

I am counted with them that go down into the pit; I am become as a man without help, free among the dead,

Like the bodies of the slain that sleep in the grave, whom Thou rememberest no more, and they are cut off from Thy hand.

They laid me in the lowest pit, in darkness and in the shadow of death.

Against me is Thine anger made strong, and all Thy billows hast Thou brought upon me.

Thou hast removed my friends afar from me; they have made me an abomination unto themselves.

I have been delivered up, and have not come forth; mine eyes are grown weak from poverty.

I have cried unto Thee, O Lord, the whole day long; I have stretched out my hands unto Thee.

Nay, for the dead wilt Thou work wonders? Or shall physicians raise them up that they may give thanks unto Thee?

Nay, shall any in the grave tell of Thy mercy, and of Thy truth in that destruction?

Nay, shall Thy wonders be known in that darkness, and Thy righteousness in that land that is forgotten?

But as for me, unto Thee, O Lord, have I cried; and in the morning shall my prayer come before Thee.

15 Wherefore, O Lord, dost Thou cast off my soul and turnest Thy face away from me?

A poor man am I, and in troubles from my youth; yea, having been exalted, I was humbled and brought to distress.

Thy furies have passed upon me, and Thy terrors have sorely troubled me.

They came round about me like water, all the day long they compassed me about together.

Thou hast removed afar from me friend and neighbour, and mine acquaintances because of my misery.

Glory. Both now. Alleluia.

PSALM LXXXVIII. 88

Concerning instruction; for Etham the Israelite.

Of Thy mercies, O Lord, will I sing for ever.

Unto generation and generation will I declare Thy truth with my mouth.

For Thou hast said: Mercy shall be built up for ever. In the heavens shall Thy truth be established.

I have made a covenant with My chosen ones, I have sworn unto David My servant: I will establish thy seed until eternity, and build up thy throne unto generation and generation.

5 The heavens shall confess Thy wonders, O Lord, and Thy truth in the congregation of saints.

For who in the clouds shall be compared unto the Lord? And who shall be likened to the Lord among the sons of God?

God Who is glorified in the council of the saints is great and terrible towards all that are round about Him.

O Lord God of hosts, who is like unto Thee? Mighty art Thou, O Lord, and Thy truth is round about Thee.

Thou art sovereign over the strength of the sea, and the tumult of her waves Thou makest calm.

10 Thou hast brought the proud man low as the corpse of one slain, and with the arm of Thy power hast Thou scattered Thine enemies.

Thine are the heavens, and Thine is the earth; the world and the fulness thereof hast Thou founded; the north and the sea hast Thou created.

Tabor and Hermon shall rejoice in Thy Name. Thine is the arm that hath might.

Let Thy hand be strengthened, let Thy right hand be lifted up on high; righteousness and judgment are the establishment of Thy throne.

Mercy and truth shall go before Thy face. Blessed is the people that knoweth jubilation.

15 O Lord, in the light of Thy face shall they walk, and in Thy Name shall they rejoice all the day long, and in Thy righteousness shall they be exalted.

For the boast of their strength art Thou, and in Thy good pleasure shall our horn be lifted high.

For from the Lord is our defence, yea, from the Holy One of Israel, our King.

At that time Thou spakest in a vision to Thy sons, and Thou didst say: I have bestowed help on one that is mighty, I have raised up one chosen out of My people.

I have found David My servant, with My holy oil have I anointed him.

For My hand shall be unto him an ally, and Mine arm shall strengthen him.

No advantage shall his enemy have over him, nor shall the son of iniquity avail to hurt him any more.

And I will hew down his enemies before his face, and them that hate him shall I put to flight.

And My truth and My mercy shall be with him, and in My Name shall his horn be lifted high.

And I will set his hand in the sea, and his right hand in the rivers.

He shall call upon Me and shall say: My Father art Thou, my God, and the helper of my salvation.

And as for Me, I will make him My firstborn, higher than the kings of the earth.

For ever shall I keep for him My mercy, and My covenant shall be faithful unto him.

And I will establish his seed unto ages of ages, and his throne shall be as the days of heaven.

If his sons forsake My law, and if they walk not in My judgments,

30 If My statutes they profane, and keep not My commandments,

I will visit their iniquities with a rod, and their injustices with scourges.

But My mercy will I not disperse away from them, nor will I wrong them in My truth.

Nor will I profane My covenant, nor the things that proceed from My lips will I make void.

Once have I sworn by My holiness that to David I will not lie; his seed for ever shall abide.

35 And his throne shall be as the sun before Me, and as the moon that is established for ever, and is a faithful witness in the sky. *(Diapsalm)*

But Thou hast cast off and brought to nought, Thou hast been wroth with Thine anointed.

Thou hast destroyed the covenant of Thy servant, Thou hast profaned his sanctuary unto the earth.

Thou hast broken down all his hedges, Thou hast made his strongholds to be his terror.

All have despoiled him that pass along the way, he is become a reproach unto his neighbours.

40 Thou hast exalted the right hand of them that afflict him, Thou hast gladdened all his enemies.

Thou hast turned away the help of his sword, and hast not helped him in the battle.

Thou hast made an end of his purification, his throne unto the earth hast Thou cast down.

Thou hast shortened the days of his time, Thou hast poured down shame upon him.

How long, O Lord, dost Thou turn away unto the end? Shall Thy wrath burn like fire?

Remember what my substance is. Nay, hast Thou created all the sons of man in vain?

Who is the man that shall live and not see death? Can he deliver his soul out of the hand of hades?

Where are Thine ancient mercies, O Lord, which Thou swarest unto David in Thy truth?

Remember, O Lord, the reproach of Thy servants, which I have endured in my bosom from many nations,

Wherewith Thine enemies have reproached, O Lord, wherewith they have reproached the recompense of Thine anointed.

Blessed is the Lord for ever. So be it. So be it.

Glory. Both now. Alleluia.

PSALM LXXXIX. 89

A prayer of Moses, the man of God.

LORD, Thou hast been our refuge in generation and generation.

Before the mountains came to be and the earth was formed and the world, even from everlasting to everlasting Thou art.

Turn not man away unto lowliness; yea, Thou hast said: Turn back, ye sons of men.

For a thousand years in Thine eyes, O Lord, are but as yesterday that is past, and as a watch in the night.

Things of no account shall their years be; in the morning like grass shall man pass away.

In the morning shall he bloom and pass away, in the evening shall he fall and grow withered and dry.

For we have fainted away in Thy wrath, and in Thine anger have we been troubled.

Thou hast set our iniquities before Thee; our lifespan is in the light of Thy countenance.

For all our days are faded away, and in Thy wrath are we fainted away; our years have, like a spider, spun out their tale.

10 As for the days of our years, in their span they be threescore years and ten.

And if we be in strength, mayhap fourscore years; and what is more than these is toil and travail.

For mildness is come upon us, and we shall be chastened.

Who knoweth the might of Thy wrath? And out of fear of Thee, who can recount Thine anger?

So make Thy right hand known to me, and to them that in their heart are instructed in wisdom.

15 Return, O Lord; how long? And be Thou entreated concerning Thy servants.

We were filled in the morning with Thy mercy, O Lord, and we rejoiced and were glad.

In all our days, let us be glad for the days wherein Thou didst humble us, for the years wherein we saw evils.

And look upon Thy servants, and upon Thy works, and do Thou guide their sons.

And let the brightness of the Lord our God be upon us, and the works of our hands do Thou guide aright upon us, yea, the work of our hands do Thou guide aright.

PSALM XC. 90

A canticle praise of David. Without superscription among the Hebrews.

H E that dwelleth in the help of the Most High shall abide in the shelter of the God of heaven.

He shall say unto the Lord: Thou art my helper and my refuge. He is my God, and I will hope in Him.

For He shall deliver thee from the snare of the hunters and from every troubling word.

With His shoulders will He overshadow thee, and under His wings shalt thou have hope.

5 With a shield will His truth encompass thee; thou shalt not be afraid for the terror by night, nor for the arrow that flieth by day,

Nor for the thing that walketh in darkness, nor for the mishap and demon of noonday.

A thousand shall fall at thy side, and ten thousand at thy right hand, but unto thee shall it not come nigh.

Only with thine eyes shalt thou behold, and thou shalt see the reward of sinners.

For Thou, O Lord, art my hope. Thou madest the Most High thy refuge;

10 No evils shall come nigh thee, and no scourge shall draw nigh unto thy dwelling.

For He shall give His angels charge over thee, to keep thee in all thy ways.

On their hands shall they bear thee up, lest at any time thou dash thy foot against a stone.

Upon the asp and basilisk shalt thou tread, and thou shalt trample upon the lion and dragon.

For he hath set his hope on Me, and I will deliver him; I will shelter him because he hath known My Name.

15 He shall cry unto Me, and I will hearken unto him. I am with him in affliction, and I will rescue him and glorify him.

With length of days will I satisfy him, and I will show him My salvation.

> Glory. Both now. Alleluia.

THE THIRTEENTH KATHISMA

PSALM XCI. 91

A canticle psalm, for the day of the Sabbath.

It is good to give praise unto the Lord, and to chant unto Thy Name, O Most High,

To proclaim in the morning Thy mercy, and Thy truth by night, on a psaltery of ten strings, with an ode upon the harp.

For Thou hast gladdened me, O Lord, by Thy deeds, and in the works of Thy hands will I rejoice.

How great are Thy works, O Lord, exceeding deep are Thy thoughts.

5   A mindless man shall not know it, nor shall a stupid man understand it.

When the sinners spring up like grass, and all that work iniquity look loftily down,

It is that they may be utterly destroyed unto ages of ages; but Thou art Most High for ever, O Lord.

For lo, Thine enemies, O Lord, for lo, Thine enemies shall perish; and scattered shall be all they that work iniquity.

And lifted high as that of a unicorn shall be my horn, and mine old age shall be strengthened with rich oil.

10   And mine eye hath looked down upon mine enemies, and mine ear shall hear concerning the wicked that rise up against me.

The righteous man shall flourish like a palm tree, and like a cedar in Lebanon shall he be multiplied.

They that are planted in the house of the Lord, in the courts of our God they shall blossom forth.

They shall still increase in a ripe old age, and happy shall they be to proclaim that upright is the Lord our God, and there is no unrighteousness in Him.

PSALM XCII. 92

A canticle praise of David: for the day before the Sabbath, when the land was first inhabited.

THE Lord is King, He is clothed with majesty; the Lord is clothed with strength and He hath girt Himself.

For He established the world which shall not be shaken.

Thy throne is prepared of old; Thou art from everlasting.

The rivers have lifted up, O Lord, the rivers have lifted up their voices.

5 The rivers will lift up their waves, at the voices of many waters.

Wonderful are the surgings of the sea, wonderful on high is the Lord.

Thy testimonies are made very sure. Holiness becometh Thy house, O Lord, unto length of days.

PSALM XCIII. 93

A psalm of David, for the fourth day of the week.

THE Lord is the God of vengeances; the God of vengeances hath spoken openly.

Be Thou exalted, O Thou that judgest the earth; render the proud their due.

How long shall sinners, O Lord, how long shall sinners boast?

How long shall they utter and speak unrighteousness, how long shall they speak, all they that work iniquity?

Thy people, O Lord, have they brought low, and to Thine inheritance have they done hurt.

Widow and orphan have they slain, and the proselyte have they murdered.

And they said: The Lord shall not see it, nor will the God of Jacob perceive it.

Understand then, ye mindless ones among the people; and ye fools, at length be wise.

He that planted the ear, shall He not hear? Or He that formed the eye, doth He not perceive?

He that chasteneth the heathen, shall He not rebuke? He that teacheth man knowledge?

The Lord knoweth the thoughts of men, that they are vain.

Blessed is the man whom Thou shalt chasten, O Lord; and out of Thy law shalt Thou instruct him,

That Thou mayest give him rest from evil days, until a pit be dug for the sinner.

For the Lord will not cast off His people, nor will He forsake His inheritance,

Until righteousness return unto judgment, and all that are upright of heart be nigh thereto.

Who will rise up for me against the evil-doers? Or who will stand up with me against the workers of iniquity?

Unless the Lord had brought me help, my soul had well nigh sojourned in hades.

Whenever I said: My foot hath slipped; Thy mercy, O Lord, brought help unto me.

According to the multitude of my sorrows in my heart, Thy consolations brought gladness unto my soul.

Let not the throne of iniquity have fellowship with Thee, which maketh mischief in the name of the law.

They shall hunt down the soul of the righteous man, and the innocent blood shall they condemn.

Yea, the Lord is become my refuge, and my God the helper of my hope.

And the Lord shall give back to them their own iniquity, and according to their wickedness the Lord God shall make them to be seen no more.

Glory. Both now. Alleluia.

PSALM XCIV. 94

A canticle praise of David. Without superscription among the Hebrews.

COME let us rejoice in the Lord, let us shout with jubilation unto God our Saviour.

Let us come before His countenance with thanksgiving, and with psalms let us shout in jubilation unto Him.

For the Lord is a great God and a great king over all the earth.

For in His hand are the ends of the earth, and the heights of the mountains are His.

For the sea is His, and He made it; and the dry land His hands have fashioned.

O come, let us worship and fall down before Him, and let us weep before the Lord Who made us.

For He is our God, and we are the people of His pasture and the sheep of His hand.

Today if ye will hear His voice, harden not your hearts, as in the provocation, in the day of temptation in the wilderness.

For your fathers tempted Me, they proved Me and saw My works.

10 Forty years long was I grieved with that generation, and I said: They do always err in their hearts.

And they have not known My ways; so I sware in Mine anger: They shall not enter into My rest.

PSALM XCV. 95

A canticle praise. David's. When the house was built after the captivity. Without superscription among the Hebrews.

O SING unto the Lord a new song, sing unto the Lord, all the earth.

Sing unto the Lord, bless His Name; proclaim from day to day the good tidings of His salvation.

Declare among the nations His glory, and among all peoples His wonders.

For great is the Lord, and greatly to be praised; He is to be feared above all gods.

5 For all the gods of the nations are demons, but the Lord made the heavens.

Praise and beauty are before Him, holiness and majesty are in His sanctuary.

Bring to the Lord, ye kindreds of the nations, bring to

the Lord glory and honour; bring to the Lord the glory due unto His Name.

Bring sacrifices, and go into His courts; worship the Lord in His holy court.

Let the earth be shaken at His presence; say among the nations that the Lord is king.

10 For He hath established the world which shall not be shaken; He shall judge the people in uprightness.

Let the heavens be glad and let the earth rejoice; let the sea be shaken, and the fulness thereof. The plains shall be joyful, and all the things therein.

Then shall all the trees of the forest rejoice at the presence of the Lord, for He cometh, for He cometh to judge the earth.

He shall judge the world with righteousness, and the peoples with His truth.

PSALM XCVI. 96

David's. When the land was restored to him.
Without superscription among the Hebrews.

THE Lord is king, let the earth rejoice; let the many islands be glad.

Clouds and darkness are round about Him; righteousness and judgment are the establishment of His throne.

Fire shall go before Him, and shall burn up His enemies round about.

His lightnings have shone forth throughout the world; the earth saw it and was shaken.

5 The mountains melted like wax at the presence of the Lord, at the presence of the Lord of all the earth.

The heavens declared His righteousness, and all the peoples saw His glory.

Let all be put to shame that worship graven things, that boast themselves of their idols.

Worship Him, all ye His angels; Sion heard and was glad,

And the daughters of Judea rejoiced because of Thy judgments, O Lord.

10 For Thou art Lord Most High over all the earth, Thou art exalted far above all the gods.

Ye that love the Lord, see to it that ye hate evil. The Lord preserveth the souls of His saints; from the hand of the sinner shall He deliver them.

A light hath dawned forth for the righteous man, and gladness for the upright of heart.

Be glad in the Lord, O ye righteous, and give thanks for the remembrance of His holiness.

Glory. Both now. Alleluia.

PSALM XCVII. 97
A psalm of David.

O SING unto the Lord a new song, for the Lord hath wrought wondrous things.

His right hand and His holy arm have wrought salvation for Him.

The Lord hath made known His salvation, in the sight of the nations hath He revealed His righteousness.

He hath remembered His mercy to Jacob, and His truth to the house of Israel.

5 All the ends of the earth have seen the salvation of our God.

Shout with jubilation unto the Lord, all the earth; sing and rejoice and chant psalms.

Chant ye unto the Lord with a harp, with the harp and with the voice of a psalm, with trumpets of metal, and with a voice of a trumpet of horn.

Shout with jubilation before the Lord our King; let the sea be shaken and the fulness thereof, the world and all they that dwell therein.

The rivers shall clap their hands together; the mountains shall rejoice at the presence of the Lord, for He cometh; yea, He is come to judge the earth.

10 He will judge the world with righteousness, and the peoples with uprightness.

PSALM XCVIII. 98

A psalm of David.

THE Lord is king, let the peoples rage; He sitteth on the cherubim, let the earth be shaken.

The Lord is great in Sion, and He is high above all peoples.

Let them confess Thy great Name, for it is terrible and holy; and the king's honour loveth judgment.

Thou hast prepared uprightness; judgment and righteousness in Jacob hast Thou wrought.

5 Exalt ye the Lord our God, and worship the footstool of His feet; for He is holy.

Moses and Aaron among His priests, and Samuel among them that call upon His Name,

They called upon the Lord, and He hearkened unto them; in a pillar of cloud He spake unto them.

For they kept His testimonies and His ordinances which He gave them.

O Lord our God, Thou didst hearken unto them; O God, Thou wast fain to be entreated for them, and yet tookest vengeance on all their devices.

10 Exalt ye the Lord our God, and worship at His holy mountain; for holy is the Lord our God.

PSALM XCIX. 99

A psalm of David; for a thank-offering.

SHOUT with jubilation unto God, all the earth; serve the Lord with gladness.

Come before His presence with rejoicing. Know ye that the Lord Himself is our God; it is He that hath made us, and not we ourselves.

We are His people and the sheep of His pasture. Enter into His gates with thanksgiving, into His courts with hymns; give thanks unto Him.

Praise His Name, for the Lord is good; His mercy endureth for ever, and His truth unto generation and generation.

PSALM C. 100

A psalm of David.

OF mercy and judgment will I sing unto Thee, O Lord; I will chant and have understanding in a blameless path. When wilt Thou come unto me?

I have walked in the innocence of my heart in the midst of my house.

I have no unlawful thing before mine eyes; the workers of transgressions I have hated.

A crooked heart hath not cleaved unto me; as for the wicked man who turned from me, I knew him not.

5 Him that privily talked against his neighbour did I drive away from me.

With him whose eye was proud and his heart insatiate, I did not eat.

Mine eyes were upon the faithful of the land, that they might sit with me; the man that walked in the blameless path, he ministered unto me.

The proud doer dwelt not in the midst of my house; the speaker of unjust things prospered not before mine eyes.

In the morning I slew all the sinners of the land, utterly to destroy out of the city of the Lord all them that work iniquity.

Glory. Both now. Alleluia.

THE FOURTEENTH KATHISMA

PSALM CI. 101

A prayer of the poor man, when he was despondent,
and poured out his supplication before the Lord.

O LORD, hear my prayer, and let my cry come unto Thee.

Turn not Thy face away from me; in the day when I am afflicted, incline Thine ear unto me.

In the day when I call upon Thee, quickly hearken unto me.

For my days are vanished like smoke, and my bones consumed like wood for the burning.

I am smitten like grass, and withered is my heart, for I forgot to eat my bread.

By reason of the voice of my groaning, my bone hath cleaved unto my flesh.

I am become like a pelican of the wilderness, I am like an owl in a ruined house.

I have watched, and am like a sparrow that sitteth alone upon the house-top.

The whole day long mine enemies reproached me, and they that praised me made an oath against me.

For before the face of Thy wrath and Thine anger I ate ashes like bread, and my drink I mingled with weeping; for after uplifting me, Thou hast dashed me down.

My days like a shadow have declined, and I like grass am withered.

But Thou, O Lord, for ever abidest, and Thy remembrance is unto generation and generation.

Thou shalt rise up and have pity upon Sion, for it is time to have compassion on her, yea, the time is come.

For Thy servants have taken pleasure in her stones, and they shall feel pity for her dust.

15 And the nations shall fear Thy Name, O Lord, and all the kings of the earth Thy glory.

For the Lord shall build up Sion, and He shall be seen in His glory.

He hath regarded the prayer of the humble, and hath not despised their supplication.

Let this be written for another generation, and the people that is being created shall praise the Lord.

For He hath looked out from His holy height, the Lord from heaven hath looked upon the earth,

20 To hear the groaning of them that be in fetters, to loose the sons of the slain,

To declare in Sion the Name of the Lord, and His praise in Jerusalem,

When the peoples are gathered together, and the kings to serve the Lord.

He answered Him in the way of his strength: The fewness of my days declare unto me.

Take me not away at the half of my days; in generations and generations are Thy years.

25 In the beginning, O Lord, Thou didst lay the foundation of the earth, and the heavens are the works of Thy hands.

They shall perish, but Thou abidest; and all like a garment shall grow old,

And as a vesture shalt Thou fold them, and they shall be changed; but Thou art the same, and Thy years shall not fail.

The sons of Thy servants shall have their dwelling, and their seed for ever shall be guided aright.

PSALM CII. 102
David's.

BLESS the Lord, O my soul, and all that is within me bless His holy Name.

Bless the Lord, O my soul, and forget not all that He hath done for thee,

Who is gracious unto all thine iniquities, Who healeth all thine infirmities,

Who redeemeth thy life from corruption, Who crowneth thee with mercy and compassion,

5   Who fulfilleth thy desire with good things; thy youth shall be renewed as the eagle's.

The Lord performeth deeds of mercy, and executeth judgment for all them that are wronged.

He hath made His ways known unto Moses, unto the sons of Israel the things that He hath willed.

Compassionate and merciful is the Lord, long-suffering and plenteous in mercy; not unto the end will He be angered, neither unto eternity will He be wroth.

Not according to our iniquities hath He dealt with us, neither according to our sins hath He rewarded us.

10 For according to the height of heaven from the earth, the Lord hath made His mercy to prevail over them that fear Him.

As far as the east is from the west, so far hath He removed our iniquities from us.

Like as a father hath compassion upon his sons, so hath the Lord had compassion upon them that fear Him; for He knoweth whereof we are made, He hath remembered that we are dust.

As for man, his days are as the grass; as a flower of the field, so shall he blossom forth.

For when the wind is passed over it, then it shall be gone, and no longer will it know the place thereof.

15 But the mercy of the Lord is from eternity, even unto eternity, upon them that fear Him.

And His righteousness is upon sons of sons, upon them that keep His testament and remember His commandments to do them.

The Lord in heaven hath prepared His throne, and His kingdom ruleth over all.

Bless the Lord, all ye His angels, mighty in strength, that perform His word, to hear the voice of His words.

Bless the Lord, all ye His hosts, His ministers that do His will.

20 Bless the Lord, all ye His works, in every place of His dominion. Bless the Lord, O my soul.

Glory. Both now. Alleluia.

PSALM CIII. 103

David's. Concerning the formation of the world.

BLESS the Lord, O my soul; O Lord my God, Thou hast been magnified exceedingly.

Confession and majesty hast Thou put on, Who coverest Thyself with light as with a garment,

Who stretchest out the heaven as it were a curtain; Who supporteth His chambers in the waters,

Who appointeth the clouds for His ascent, Who walketh upon the wings of the winds,

5   Who maketh His angels spirits, and His ministers a flame of fire,

Who establisheth the earth in the sureness thereof; it shall not be turned back for ever and ever.

The abyss like a garment is His mantle; upon the mountains shall the waters stand.

At Thy rebuke they will flee, at the voice of Thy thunder shall they be afraid.

The mountains rise up and the plains sink down, unto the place where Thou hast established them.

10   Thou appointedst a bound that they shall not pass, neither return to cover the earth.

He sendeth forth springs in the valleys; between the mountains will the waters run.

They shall give drink to all the beasts of the field; the wild asses will wait to quench their thirst.

Beside them will the birds of the heaven lodge, from the midst of the rocks will they give voice.

He watereth the mountains from His chambers; the earth shall be satisfied with the fruit of Thy works.

15. He causeth the grass to grow for the cattle, and green herb for the service of men,

To bring forth bread out of the earth; and wine maketh glad the heart of man.

To make his face cheerful with oil; and bread strengtheneth man's heart.

The trees of the plain shall be satisfied, the cedars of Lebanon, which Thou hast planted.

There will the sparrows make their nests; the house of the heron is chief among them.

20. The high mountains are a refuge for the harts, and so is the rock for the hares.

He hath made the moon for seasons; the sun knoweth his going down.

Thou appointedst the darkness, and there was the night, wherein all the beasts of the forest will go abroad.

Young lions roaring after their prey, and seeking their food from God.

The sun ariseth, and they are gathered together, and they lay them down in their dens.

25. But man shall go forth unto his work, and to his labour until the evening.

How magnified are Thy works, O Lord! In wisdom hast Thou made them all; the earth is filled with Thy creation.

So is this great and spacious sea, therein are things creeping innumerable, small living creatures with the great.

There go the ships; there this dragon, whom Thou hast made to play therein.

All things wait on Thee, to give them their food in due season; when Thou givest it them, they will gather it.

When Thou openest Thy hand, all things shall be filled with goodness; when Thou turnest away Thy face, they shall be troubled.

Thou wilt take their spirit, and they shall cease; and unto their dust shall they return.

Thou wilt send forth Thy Spirit, and they shall be created; and Thou shalt renew the face of the earth.

Let the glory of the Lord be unto the ages; the Lord will rejoice in His works,

Who looketh on the earth and maketh it tremble, Who toucheth the mountains and they smoke.

I will sing unto the Lord throughout my life, I will chant to my God for as long as I have my being.

May my words be sweet unto Him, and I will rejoice in the Lord.

O that sinners would cease from the earth, and they that work iniquity, that they should be no more. Bless the Lord, O my soul.

Glory. Both now. Alleluia.

PSALM CIV. 104

Alleluia.

O GIVE thanks unto the Lord and call upon His Name; declare among the nations His works.

Sing unto Him and chant unto Him; tell forth all His wonders.

Glory in His holy Name; let the heart of them be glad that seek the Lord.

Seek ye the Lord, and be strengthened; seek ye His face at all times.

5 Remember His wonders which He wrought, His marvels, and the judgments of His mouth,

Ye that are the seed of Abraham, His servants, ye sons of Jacob, His chosen.

He is the Lord our God, in all the earth are His judgments.

He hath remembered His covenant unto eternity, the word which He commanded unto a thousand generations,

Which He made to Abraham, and His oath to Isaac.

10 And He established it to Jacob for an ordinance, and to Israel for an everlasting covenant,

Saying: Unto thee will I give the land of Canaan, the portion of your inheritance.

When they were few in number, very few and sojourners therein,

And they went from nation to nation, and from one kingdom to another people,

He allowed no man to wrong them; and He reproved kings for their sake,

15 Saying: Touch not Mine anointed ones, and to My prophets do no evil.

And He called a famine upon the land, He brake all the staff of bread.

He sent a man before them, Joseph was sold for a slave.

They humbled his feet with fetters, his life was spent in irons, until his word came to pass.

The oracle of the Lord proved him; the king sent and loosed him, even the ruler of the people, and released him.

20   He made him lord of his house, and ruler over all his substance,

To instruct his princes as himself, and to teach his elders wisdom.

And Israel went into Egypt, and Jacob sojourned in the land of Ham.

And He increased His people greatly, and made them stronger than their enemies.

He turned their heart to hate His people, to deal craftily with His servants.

25   He sent forth Moses His servant, Aaron whom He had chosen for Himself.

He set in them the words of His signs and of His marvels in the land of Ham.

He sent forth darkness and made it dark, for they were embittered against His words.

He turned their waters into blood, and He slew their fish.

Their land teemed with frogs, even unto the secret chambers of their kings.

30   He spake, and the dog-fly came, and gnats in all their borders.

He gave them hail for rain, flaming fire in their land.

And He smote their vines and their fig trees, and brake every tree of their border.

He spake, and the locust came, and the caterpillar, and that without number,

And devoured all the grass in their land, and devoured all the fruit of their land.

35 And He smote every firstborn of their land, the firstlings of all their labour.

And He led them out with silver and gold, and there was not among their tribes one man that was feeble.

Egypt was glad when they departed, for fear of them had fallen upon them.

He spread out a cloud for a shelter to them, and a fire to give them light by night.

They made request and the quail came, and with the bread of heaven He filled them.

40 He clave the rock and the waters flowed, in waterless places rivers ran.

For He remembered His holy word which He spake unto Abraham His servant.

And He led forth His people with rejoicing, and His chosen ones with gladness.

And He gave unto them the lands of the heathen, and the labours of peoples they inherited,

That they might keep His statutes and might seek after His law.

        Glory. Both now. Alleluia.

THE FIFTEENTH KATHISMA

PSALM CV. 105

Alleluia.

O GIVE thanks unto the Lord, for He is good, for His mercy endureth for ever.

Who shall tell of the mighty acts of the Lord? Who shall make all His praises to be heard?

Blessed are they that keep judgment and do righteousness at all times.

Remember us, O Lord, in Thy favour for Thy people; visit us with Thy salvation,

That we may see it in the goodness of Thy chosen, that we may be glad in the gladness of Thy nation, that we may glory with Thine inheritance.

We have sinned with our fathers, we have done iniquity, we have done unrighteousness.

Our fathers in Egypt understood not Thy wonders, and they remembered not the multitude of Thy mercy.

And they embittered Thee as they went up by the Red Sea.

And He saved them for His Name's sake, that He might make known His mighty power.

And He rebuked the Red Sea, and it was dried up; and He led them into the deep as in a wilderness.

And He saved them from the hand of him that hated them, and redeemed them from the hand of enemies.

The waters covered their oppressors; not one of them was left.

And they believed His word, and they sang His praise.

They made haste, they forgot His works, they awaited not His counsel.

15 And they desired a desire in the wilderness, and made trial of God in the waterless place.

And He gave them their request, and sent forth fulness into their souls.

And they provoked Moses in the camp, and Aaron the holy one of the Lord.

The earth opened and swallowed up Dathan, and covered over the congregation of Abiron.

And a fire was kindled in their congregation, a flame burned up the sinners.

20 And they made a calf in Horeb, and they worshipped the graven thing.

And they changed His glory into the likeness of a calf that eateth grass.

And they forgot God Who had saved them, Who had done great things in Egypt, wonders in the land of Ham, terrible things at the Red Sea.

And He said that He would destroy them, had not Moses His chosen stood in the breach before Him, to turn away His wrath, lest He should destroy them.

And they set at nought the desirable land; they believed not His word.

25 And they murmured in their tents; they hearkened not unto the voice of the Lord.

And He lifted up His hand against them, to cast them down in the wilderness,

To cast down their seed among the nations, and to scatter them in the lands.

And they were made initiates of Baal-phegor, and ate the sacrifices of the dead.

And they provoked Him with their inventions, and destruction was multiplied among them.

30 And Phineas stood up and made appeasement; and the plague abated.

And it was counted unto him for righteousness, unto generation and generation for evermore.

And they provoked Him at the water of gainsaying, and Moses suffered hurt for their sakes; for they embittered his spirit, and he gave judgment with his lips.

They did not destroy the heathen, concerning which the Lord had spoken to them.

They mingled among the nations and learned their works; and they served their graven things, and it became for them a stumbling-block.

35 And they sacrificed their sons and their daughters unto demons.

And they poured out innocent blood, the blood of their sons and daughters, whom they sacrificed to the graven things of Canaan.

And the land was befouled with the blood of murder, and it was defiled with their works; and they went a whoring with their own inventions.

And with anger was the Lord wroth against His people, and He abhorred His inheritance.

And He gave them into the hands of enemies, and they that hated them were lords over them.

40 And their enemies afflicted them, and they were humbled under their hands.

Many times He delivered them; but they embittered Him with their counsel, and they were humbled in their iniquities.

And the Lord saw when they were in affliction, when He hearkened unto their supplication.

And He remembered His covenant and repented according to the multitude of His mercy.

And He caused them to be pitied in the sight of all that had taken them captive.

45 Save us, O Lord our God, and gather us from among the nations,

That we may confess Thy holy Name, that we may glory in Thy praise.

Blessed is the Lord God of Israel, from everlasting to everlasting; and all the peoples shall say: So be it. So be it.

Glory. Both now. Alleluia.

PSALM CVI. 106

Alleluia.

O GIVE thanks unto the Lord, for He is good, for His mercy endureth for ever.

So let them say that have been redeemed by the Lord, whom He hath redeemed from the hand of the enemy.

From the lands hath He gathered them, from the east, from the west, from the north, and from the sea.

They wandered in the wilderness, in a waterless land; they found not the path to a city of habitation.

  Hungering and thirsting, their soul within them fainted.

  And they cried unto the Lord in their affliction, and out of their distresses He delivered them.

  And He guided them into the right way that they might go to a city for habitation.

  Let them give thanks unto the Lord for His mercies, and for His wondrous works for the sons of men.

  For He satisfied the empty soul, and the hungry soul hath He filled with good things.

  As for them that sit in darkness and the shadow of death, fettered with beggary and iron,

  Because they were embittered against the sayings of God and provoked the counsel of the Most High,

  Yea, with labours was their heart brought low; they waxed feeble, and there was none to help.

  And they cried unto the Lord in their affliction, and out of their distresses He saved them.

  And He brought them out of darkness and the shadow of death, and their bonds He brake asunder.

  Let them give thanks unto the Lord for His mercies, and for His wondrous works for the sons of men.

  For He shattered the gates of brass, and brake the bars of iron.

  He helped them out of the way of their lawlessness; for on account of their iniquities had they been brought low.

  All food did their soul abhor, and they drew nigh even unto the gates of death.

  And they cried unto the Lord in their affliction, and out of their distresses He saved them.

20 He sent forth His Word and He healed them, and He delivered them from their corruption.

Let them give thanks unto the Lord for His mercies, and for His wondrous works for the sons of men.

And let them sacrifice to Him a sacrifice of praise, and let them proclaim His works with rejoicing.

They that go down to the sea in ships, doing their work in many waters,

These have seen the works of the Lord, and His wonders in the deep.

25 He spake, and a wind of tempest arose, and the waves thereof were lifted up.

They mount as high as the heavens, and they go down into the abysses; their soul was melted with evils.

They were troubled, and they reeled like one drunken, and all their wisdom was swallowed up.

And they cried unto the Lord in their affliction, and out of their distresses He brought them.

And He commanded the tempest, and it was calmed into a breeze, and the waves thereof fell silent.

30 And they were glad, because they were quiet, and He guided them to the haven of His will.

Let them give thanks unto the Lord for His mercies, and for His wondrous works for the sons of men.

Let them exalt Him in the assembly of the people, and in the seat of the elders let them praise Him.

He turned rivers into a wilderness, and the coursings of waters into a thirsting land,

A fruitful land into saltiness, for the wickedness of them that dwell therein.

³⁵ He turned a wilderness into pools of waters, and a parched land into streams of water.

And He made the hungry to dwell therein, and they established cities for habitation.

And they sowed fields and planted vineyards, and they made fruits of increase.

And He blessed them and they were multiplied greatly, and He diminished not the number of their cattle.

And again they became few and were brought low by affliction, evils and sorrows.

⁴⁰ Contempt was poured out upon their princes, and He caused them to wander in a land untrodden, where there is no way.

And He helped the poor man out of his poverty, and made his kindred like a flock.

The upright shall see it and shall be glad, and all iniquity shall stop its mouth.

Who is wise and will keep these things, and will understand the mercies of the Lord?

Glory. Both now. Alleluia.

PSALM CVII. 107
A psalmic ode of David.

READY is my heart, O God, ready is my heart; I will sing and chant in my glory.

Awake, O my glory; awake, O psaltery and harp; I myself will awake at dawn.

I will confess Thee among the peoples, O Lord, I will chant unto Thee among the nations.

For great above the heavens is Thy mercy, and even unto the clouds is Thy truth.

5 Be Thou exalted above the heavens, O God, and Thy glory above all the earth.

That Thy beloved ones may be delivered, save Thou with Thy right hand and hearken unto me.

God hath spoken in His sanctuary: I will be exalted, and I will divide Sikima, and the vale of tabernacles will I measure out.

Mine is Galaad, and Mine is Manasses, and Ephraim is the protection of My head.

Judah is My king, Moab is the cauldron of My hope.

10 Upon Idumea will I stretch out My shoe; the foreign tribes have been subjected unto Me.

Who will bring me into a fortified city? Or who will lead me into Idumea?

Wilt Thou not, O God, Who hast spurned us? And wilt Thou not, O God, go forth with our forces?

Give us help from affliction, for vain is the salvation of man.

In God we shall work mighty deeds, and He will bring to nought our enemies.

PSALM CVIII. 108

For the end: a psalm of David.

O GOD, my praise do not pass over in silence; for the mouth of the sinner and the mouth of the deceitful man are opened against me.

They have spoken against me with a deceitful tongue,

and with words of hatred have they encompassed me, and they have warred against me without a cause.

In return for my love, they have falsely accused me; but as for me, I gave myself to prayer.

And they repaid me evil for good, and hatred for my love.

5 Set Thou a sinner over him, and let the devil stand at his right hand.

When he is judged, let him go forth condemned, and let his prayer become sin.

Let his days be few, and his bishopric let another take.

Let his children be fatherless, and his wife a widow.

Let his children be vagabonds without a dwelling-place, and let them beg; let them be cast out from their ruined dwellings.

10 Let his creditor search out all his substance, and let strangers plunder all his labours.

Let there be for him no helper, nor anyone to pity his fatherless children.

Let his children be given over to utter destruction; in a single generation let his name be blotted out.

Let the iniquity of his fathers be remembered before the Lord, and let not the sin of his mother be blotted out.

Let them be before the Lord continually, and let the memory of them perish from off the earth,

15 Because he remembered not to show mercy; and persecuted a man that was poor and a beggar, and one broken in heart, that he might slay him.

And he loved cursing, and it shall come upon him; and he delighted not in blessing, and it shall be far from him.

And he put on cursing like a garment, and it went in like water into his bowels, and like oil into his bones.

Let it be for him like a garment wherewith he is clothed, and like a girdle wherewith continually he is girded.

This is the dealing of the Lord with them that slander me, and with them that speak evil things against my soul.

But Thou, O Lord, O Lord, deal Thou with me for Thy Name's sake; for Thy mercy is good.

Deliver me, for a poor man am I and a pauper, and my heart is troubled within me.

Like a shadow when it declineth am I taken away, I am shaken off as the locusts.

My knees are grown weak through fasting, and my flesh is changed for want of oil.

And I am become a reproach unto them; they saw me and wagged their heads.

Help me, O Lord my God, and save me according to Thy mercy.

And let them know that this is Thy hand and that Thou, O Lord, hast wrought it.

They will curse, and Thou wilt bless; let them that rise up against me be put to shame, but Thy servant shall be glad.

Let them that slander me be clothed with confusion, and let them be covered with shame as with a mantle.

I will greatly praise the Lord with my mouth, and in the midst of many will I praise Him.

For He hath stood at the right hand of the poor, to save my soul from them that persecute me.

    Glory. Both now. Alleluia.

THE SIXTEENTH KATHISMA

PSALM CIX. 109

A psalm of David.

THE Lord said unto my Lord: Sit Thou at My right hand, until I make Thine enemies the footstool of Thy feet.

A sceptre of power shall the Lord send unto Thee out of Sion; rule Thou in the midst of Thine enemies.

With Thee is dominion in the day of Thy power, in the splendour of Thy saints.

From the womb before the morning star have I begotten Thee. The Lord hath sworn and will not repent: Thou art a priest for ever, after the order of Melchisedek.

The Lord at Thy right hand hath broken kings in the day of His wrath.

He shall judge among the nations, He shall fill them with dead bodies, He shall crush the heads of many upon the earth.

He shall drink of the brook in the way; therefore shall He lift up His head.

PSALM CX. 110

Alleluia.

I WILL confess Thee, O Lord, with my whole heart, in the council of the upright and in the congregation.

Great are the works of the Lord, sought out in all the things that He hath willed.

Confession and majesty are His work, and His righteousness abideth unto ages of ages.

He made a remembrance of His wondrous deeds; merciful and compassionate is the Lord; He hath given food to them that fear Him.

5 He will be mindful for ever of His covenant; the power of His works hath He declared unto His people,

That He may give them the inheritance of the nations; the works of His hands are truth and judgment.

Faithful are all His commandments, confirmed unto ages of ages, made in truth and uprightness.

He hath sent redemption unto His people, He hath enjoined His covenant for ever; holy and terrible is His Name.

The fear of the Lord is the beginning of wisdom; and all they that foster this have a good understanding.

10 His praise abideth unto ages of ages.

PSALM CXI. 111

Alleluia.

BLESSED is the man that feareth the Lord; in His commandments shall he greatly delight.

His seed shall be mighty upon the earth; the generation of the upright shall be blessed.

Glory and riches shall be in his house, and his righteousness abideth unto ages of ages.

There hath risen up in darkness a light for the upright; he is merciful and compassionate and righteous.

5 A good man is he that is compassionate and lendeth; he shall order his words with judgment, for he shall remain unshaken for ever.

In everlasting remembrance shall the righteous be; he shall not be afraid of evil tidings.

His heart is ready to hope in the Lord; his heart is established, he shall not be afraid, until he look down upon his enemies.

He hath dispersed, he hath given to the poor, his righteousness abideth unto ages of ages; his horn shall be exalted with glory.

The sinner shall see and be angered, he shall gnash with his teeth and melt away; the desire of the sinner shall perish.

Glory. Both now. Alleluia.

PSALM CXII. 112

Alleluia.

PRAISE the Lord, O ye servants, praise ye the Name of the Lord.

Blessed be the Name of the Lord from henceforth and for evermore.

From the rising of the sun unto the going down of the same, the Name of the Lord is to be praised.

High above all the nations is the Lord, above the heavens is His glory.

Who is like unto the Lord our God? Who dwelleth on high and looketh down on things that are lowly, in heaven and on the earth,

Who raiseth up the poor man from the earth, and from the dunghill lifteth up the pauper,

That He may seat him with princes, with the princes of His people,

Who maketh the barren woman to dwell in a house and be a mother rejoicing over children.

PSALM CXIII. 113
Alleluia.

WHEN Israel went out of Egypt, and the house of Jacob from among a barbarous people,

Judea became His sanctuary, Israel His dominion.

The sea beheld and fled, Jordan turned back.

The mountains skipped like rams, and the hills like lambs of flocks.

5 What aileth thee, O sea, that thou fleddest? And thou Jordan, that thou didst turn back?

Ye mountains, that ye skipped like rams, and ye hills like lambs of flocks?

At the presence of the Lord the earth was shaken, at the presence of the God of Jacob,

Who turneth the rock into pools of waters, and the precipice into fountains of waters.

Not unto us, O Lord, not unto us, but unto Thy Name give glory, for Thy mercy and Thy truth,

10 Lest haply the heathen say: Where is their God?

But our God is in heaven and on earth; all things soever He hath willed, He hath done.

The idols of the nations are of silver and gold, the works of the hands of men.

They have a mouth, but shall not speak; eyes have they, and shall not see.

Ears have they, and shall not hear; noses have they, and shall not smell.

15 Hands they have, and shall not feel; feet have they, and shall not walk; they shall make no sound in their throat.

Let those that make them become like unto them, and all that put their trust in them.

The house of Israel hath hoped in the Lord; their helper and defender is He.

The house of Aaron hath hoped in the Lord; their helper and defender is He.

They that fear the Lord have hoped in the Lord; their helper and defender is He.

The Lord being mindful of us, hath blessed us.

He hath blessed the house of Israel, He hath blessed the house of Aaron.

He hath blessed them that fear the Lord, the little with the great.

The Lord grant you increase, to you and to your children.

Ye are blessed of the Lord, Who made heaven and the earth.

The heaven of heaven belongeth to the Lord, but the earth He gave unto the sons of men.

Not the dead shall praise Thee, O Lord, nor any that go down to hades.

But we the living will bless the Lord from henceforth and for evermore.

PSALM CXIV. 114

Alleluia.

I AM filled with love, for the Lord will hear the voice of my supplication.

For He hath inclined His ear unto me, and in my days will I call upon Him.

The pangs of death have encompassed me, the perils of hades have found me.

Tribulation and sorrow have I found, and I called upon the Name of the Lord: O Lord, deliver my soul.

5 Merciful is the Lord and righteous, and our God hath mercy.

The Lord preserveth the infants; I was brought low and He saved me.

Return, O my soul, unto thy rest, for the Lord hath dealt bountifully with thee.

For He hath delivered my soul from death, mine eyes from tears, and my feet from sliding.

I will be well-pleasing before the Lord in the land of the living.

Glory. Both now. Alleluia.

PSALM CXV. 115

Alleluia.

I BELIEVED, wherefore I spake; I was humbled exceedingly.

As for me, I said in mine ecstasy: Every man is a liar.

What shall I render unto the Lord for all that He hath rendered unto me?

I will take the cup of salvation, and I will call upon the Name of the Lord.

5 My vows unto the Lord will I pay in the presence of all His people.

Precious in the sight of the Lord is the death of His saints.

O Lord, I am Thy servant; I am Thy servant and the

son of Thy handmaid. Thou hast broken my bonds asunder.

I will sacrifice a sacrifice of praise unto Thee, and I will call upon the Name of the Lord.

My vows unto the Lord will I pay in the presence of all His people, in the courts of the house of the Lord, in the midst of thee, O Jerusalem.

PSALM CXVI. 116
Alleluia.

O PRAISE the Lord, all ye nations; praise Him, all ye peoples.

For He hath made His mercy to prevail over us, and the truth of the Lord abideth for ever.

PSALM CXVII. 117
Alleluia.

O GIVE thanks unto the Lord, for He is good, for His mercy endureth for ever.

Let the house of Israel now say that He is good, for His mercy endureth for ever.

Let the house of Aaron now say that He is good, for His mercy endureth for ever.

Let all that fear the Lord now say that He is good, for His mercy endureth for ever.

5 Out of mine affliction I called upon the Lord, and He heard me and brought me into a broad place.

The Lord is my helper, and I will not fear what man shall do unto me.

The Lord is my helper, and I shall look down upon mine enemies.

It is better to trust in the Lord than to trust in man.

It is better to hope in the Lord than to hope in princes.

All the nations compassed me round about, and by the Name of the Lord I warded them off.

Surrounding me they compassed me, and by the Name of the Lord I warded them off.

They compassed me about like unto bees around a honeycomb, and they burst into flame like a fire among the thorns, and by the Name of the Lord I warded them off.

I was pushed and overturned that I might fall, and the Lord was quick to help me.

The Lord is my strength and my song, and He is become my salvation.

The voice of rejoicing and salvation is in the tents of the righteous.

The right hand of the Lord hath wrought strength, the right hand of the Lord hath exalted me, the right hand of the Lord hath wrought strength.

I shall not die, but live, and I shall tell of the works of the Lord.

With chastisement hath the Lord chastened me, but He hath not given me over unto death.

Open unto me the gates of righteousness; I will enter therein and give thanks unto the Lord.

This is the gate of the Lord, the righteous shall enter in thereat.

I will give thanks unto Thee, for Thou hast heard me and art become my salvation.

The stone which the builders rejected, the same is become the head of the corner.

This is the Lord's doing, and it is marvellous in our eyes.

This is the day which the Lord hath made; let us rejoice and be glad therein.

O Lord, save now; O Lord, send now prosperity. Blessed is he that cometh in the Name of the Lord.

We have blessed you out of the house of the Lord. God is the Lord, and hath appeared unto us.

Ordain a feast with thick boughs, even unto the horns of the altar.

Thou art my God, and I will confess Thee; Thou art my God, and I will exalt Thee.

I will give thanks unto Thee, for Thou hast heard me, and Thou art become my salvation.

O give thanks unto the Lord, for He is good, for His mercy endureth for ever.

Glory. Both now. Alleluia.

THE SEVENTEENTH KATHISMA

PSALM CXVIII. 118

Alleluia.

BLESSED are the blameless in the way, who walk in the law of the Lord.

Blessed are they that search out His testimonies; with their whole heart shall they seek after Him.

For they that work iniquity have not walked in His ways.

Thou hast enjoined Thy commandments, that we should keep them most diligently.

Would that my ways were directed to keep Thy statutes.

Then shall I not be ashamed, when I look on all Thy commandments.

I will confess Thee with uprightness of heart, when I have learned the judgments of Thy righteousness.

I will keep Thy statutes; do not utterly forsake me.

Wherewithal shall a young man correct his way? By keeping Thy words.

With my whole heart have I sought after Thee, cast me not away from Thy commandments.

In my heart have I hid Thy sayings that I might not sin against Thee.

Blessed art Thou, O Lord, teach me Thy statutes.

With my lips have I declared all the judgments of Thy mouth.

In the way of Thy testimonies have I found delight, as much as in all riches.

15 On Thy commandments will I ponder, and I will understand Thy ways.

On Thy statutes will I meditate; I will not forget Thy words.

Give reward unto Thy servant, quicken me and I will keep Thy words.

O unveil mine eyes, and I shall perceive wondrous things out of Thy law.

I am a sojourner on the earth, hide not from me Thy commandments.

20 My soul hath longed to desire Thy judgments at all times.

Thou hast rebuked the proud; cursed are they that decline from Thy commandments.

Remove from me reproach and contempt, for after Thy testimonies have I sought.

For princes sat and they spake against me, but Thy servant pondered on Thy statutes.

For Thy testimonies are my meditation, and Thy statutes are my counsellors.

25 My soul hath cleaved unto the earth; quicken me according to Thy word.

My ways have I declared, and Thou hast heard me; teach me Thy statutes.

Make me to understand the way of Thy statutes, and I will ponder on Thy wondrous works.

My soul hath slumbered from despondency, strengthen me with Thy words.

Remove from me the way of unrighteousness, and with Thy law have mercy on me.

30 I have chosen the way of truth, and Thy judgments have I not forgotten.

I have cleaved to Thy testimonies, O Lord; put me not to shame.

The way of Thy commandments have I run, when Thou didst enlarge my heart.

Set before me for a law, O Lord, the way of Thy statutes, and I will seek after it continually.

Give me understanding, and I will search out Thy law, and I will keep it with my whole heart.

35 Guide me in the path of Thy commandments, for I have desired it.

Incline my heart unto Thy testimonies and not unto covetousness.

Turn away mine eyes that I may not see vanity, quicken Thou me in Thy way.

Establish for Thy servant Thine oracle unto fear of Thee.

Remove my reproach which I have feared, for Thy judgments are good.

40 Behold, I have longed after Thy commandments; in Thy righteousness quicken me.

Let Thy mercy come also upon me, O Lord, even Thy salvation according to Thy word.

So shall I give an answer to them that reproach me, for I have hoped in Thy words.

And take not utterly out of my mouth the word of truth, for in Thy judgments have I hoped.

So shall I keep Thy law continually, for ever, and unto the ages of ages.

45 And I walked in spaciousness, for after Thy commandments have I sought.

And I spake of Thy testimonies before kings, and I was not ashamed.

And I meditated on Thy commandments which I have greatly loved.

And I lifted up my hands to Thy commandments which I have loved, and I pondered on Thy statutes.

Remember Thy words to Thy servant, wherein Thou hast made me to hope.

50 This hath comforted me in my humiliation, for Thine oracle hath quickened me.

The proud have transgressed exceedingly, but from Thy law have I not declined.

I remembered Thy judgments of old, O Lord, and was comforted.

Despondency took hold upon me because of the sinners who forsake Thy law.

Thy statutes were my songs in the place of my sojourning.

55 I remembered Thy Name in the night, O Lord, and I kept Thy law.

This hath happened unto me because I sought after Thy statutes.

Thou art my portion, O Lord; I said that I would keep Thy law.

I entreated Thy countenance with my whole heart: Have mercy on me according to Thy word.

I have thought on Thy ways, and I have turned my feet back to Thy testimonies.

60 I made ready, and I was not troubled, that I might keep Thy commandments.

The cords of sinners have entangled me, but Thy law have I not forgotten.

At midnight I arose to give thanks unto Thee for the judgments of Thy righteousness.

I am a partaker with all them that fear Thee, and with them that keep Thy commandments.

The earth, O Lord, is full of Thy mercy; teach me Thy statutes.

65 Thou hast dealt graciously with Thy servant, O Lord, according to Thy word.

Goodness and discipline and knowledge teach Thou me, for in Thy commandments have I believed.

Before I was humbled, I transgressed; therefore Thy saying have I kept.

Thou art good, O Lord, and in Thy goodness teach me Thy statutes.

Multiplied against me hath been the unrighteousness of the proud; but as for me, with my whole heart will I search out Thy commandments.

70 Curdled like milk is their heart; but as for me, in Thy law have I meditated.

It is good for me that Thou hast humbled me, that I might learn Thy statutes.

The law of Thy mouth is better to me than thousands of gold and silver.

Glory. Both now. Alleluia.

SECOND STASIS

Thy hands have made me and fashioned me; give me understanding and I will learn Thy commandments.

They that fear Thee shall see me and be glad, for on Thy words have I set my hope.

I have known, O Lord, that Thy judgments are righteousness, and with truth hast Thou humbled me.

Let now Thy mercy be my comfort, according to Thy saying unto Thy servant.

Let Thy compassions come upon me and I shall live, for Thy law is my meditation.

Let the proud be put to shame, for unjustly have they transgressed against me; but as for me, I will ponder on Thy commandments.

Let those that fear Thee return unto me, and those that know Thy testimonies.

Let my heart be blameless in Thy statutes, that I may not be put to shame.

My soul fainteth for Thy salvation; on Thy words have I set my hope.

Mine eyes are grown dim with waiting for Thine oracle; they say: When wilt Thou comfort me?

For I am become like a wine-skin in the frost; yet Thy statutes have I not forgotten.

How many are the days of Thy servant? When wilt Thou execute judgment for me on them that persecute me?

Transgressors have told me fables, but they are not like Thy law, O Lord.

All Thy commandments are truth. Without a cause have men persecuted me; do Thou help me.

They well nigh made an end of me on the earth; but as for me, I forsook not Thy commandments.

According to Thy mercy quicken me, and I will keep the testimonies of Thy mouth.

For ever, O Lord, Thy word abideth in heaven.

90 Unto generation and generation is Thy truth; Thou hast laid the foundation of the earth, and it abideth.

By Thine ordinance doth the day abide, for all things are Thy servants.

If Thy law had not been my meditation, then should I have perished in my humiliation.

I will never forget Thy statutes, for in them hast Thou quickened me.

MIDDLE

I am Thine, save me; for after Thy statutes have I sought.

95 Sinners have waited for me to destroy me; but Thy testimonies have I understood.

Of all perfection have I seen the outcome; exceeding spacious is Thy commandment.

O how I have loved Thy law, O Lord! the whole day long it is my meditation.

Above mine enemies hast Thou made me wise in Thy commandment, for it is mine for ever.

Above all that teach me have I gained understanding, for Thy testimonies are my meditation.

100   Above mine elders have I received understanding, for after Thy commandments have I sought.

From every way that is evil have I restrained my feet that I might keep Thy words.

From Thy judgments have I not declined, for Thou hast set a law for me.

How sweet to my palate are Thy sayings! more sweet than honey to my mouth.

From Thy commandments have I gained understanding; therefore have I hated every way of unrighteousness.

105   Thy law is a lamp unto my feet and a light unto my paths.

I have sworn and resolved that I will keep the judgments of Thy righteousness.

I was humbled exceedingly; O Lord, quicken me according to Thy word.

The free-will offerings of my mouth be Thou now pleased to receive, O Lord, and teach me Thy judgments.

My soul is in Thy hands continually, and Thy law have I not forgotten.

110   Sinners have set a snare for me, yet from Thy commandment have I not strayed.

I have inherited Thy testimonies for ever, for they are the rejoicing of my heart.

I have inclined my heart to perform Thy statutes for ever for a recompense.

Transgressors have I hated, but Thy law have I loved.

My helper and my protector art Thou; on Thy words have I set my hope.

115   Depart from me, ye evil-doers, and I will search out the commandments of my God.

Uphold me according to Thy saying and quicken me, and turn me not away in shame from mine expectation.

Help me, and I shall be saved; and I will meditate on Thy statutes continually.

Thou hast set at nought all that depart from Thy statutes, for unrighteous is their inward thought.

I have reckoned as transgressors all the sinners of the earth, therefore have I loved Thy testimonies.

120   Nail down my flesh with the fear of Thee, for of Thy judgments am I afraid.

I have wrought judgment and righteousness; O give me not up to them that wrong me.

Receive Thy servant unto good, let not the proud falsely accuse me.

Mine eyes have failed with waiting for Thy salvation, and for the word of Thy righteousness.

Deal with Thy servant according to Thy mercy, and teach me Thy statutes.

125   I am Thy servant; give me understanding, and I shall know Thy testimonies.

It is time for the Lord to act; for they have dispersed Thy law.

Therefore have I loved Thy commandments more than gold and topaz.

Therefore I directed myself according to all Thy commandments; every way that is unrighteous have I hated.

Wonderful are Thy testimonies; therefore hath my soul searched them out.

130 The unfolding of Thy words will give light and understanding unto babes.

I opened my mouth and drew in my breath, for I longed for Thy commandments.

> Glory. Both now. Alleluia.

THIRD STASIS

Look upon me and have mercy on me, according to the judgment of them that love Thy Name.

My steps do Thou direct according to Thy saying, and let no iniquity have dominion over me.

Deliver me from the false accusation of men, and I will keep Thy commandments.

135 Make Thy face to shine upon Thy servant, and teach me Thy statutes.

Mine eyes have poured forth streams of waters, because I kept not Thy law.

Righteous art Thou, O Lord, and upright are Thy judgments.

Thou hast ordained as Thy testimonies exceeding righteousness and truth.

My zeal for Thee hath made me to pine away, because mine enemies have forgotten Thy words.

140 Thine oracle is tried with fire to the uttermost, and Thy servant hath loved it.

I am young and accounted as nothing, yet Thy statutes have I not forgotten.

Thy righteousness is an everlasting righteousness, and Thy law is truth.

Tribulations and necessities have found me, Thy commandments are my meditation.

Thy testimonies are righteousness for ever; give me understanding and I shall live.

145 I have cried with my whole heart; hear me, O Lord, and I will seek after Thy statutes.

I have cried unto Thee; save me, and I will keep Thy testimonies.

I arose in the dead of night and I cried; on Thy words have I set my hope.

Mine eyes woke before the morning that I might meditate on Thy sayings.

Hear my voice, O Lord, according to Thy mercy; according to Thy judgment, quicken me.

150 They have drawn nigh that lawlessly persecute me, but from Thy law are they far removed.

Near art Thou, O Lord, and all Thy ways are truth.

From the beginning I have known from Thy testimonies that Thou hast founded them for ever.

Behold my humiliation and rescue me, for Thy law have I not forgotten.

Judge my cause and redeem me; for Thy word's sake quicken me.

155 Far from sinners is salvation, for they have not sought after Thy statutes.

Thy compassions are many, O Lord; according to Thy judgment quicken me.

Many are they that persecute me and afflict me; from Thy testimonies have I not declined.

I beheld men acting foolishly and I pined away, because they kept not Thy sayings.

Behold, how I have loved Thy commandments; O Lord, in Thy mercy, quicken me.

The beginning of Thy words is truth, and all the judgments of Thy righteousness endure for ever.

Princes have persecuted me without a cause, and because of Thy words my heart hath been afraid.

I will rejoice in Thy sayings as one that findeth great spoil.

Unrighteousness have I hated and abhorred, but Thy law have I loved.

Seven times a day have I praised Thee for the judgments of Thy righteousness.

Much peace have they that love Thy law, and for them there is no stumbling-block.

I awaited Thy salvation, O Lord, and Thy commandments have I loved.

My soul hath kept Thy testimonies and hath loved them exceedingly.

I have kept Thy commandments and Thy testimonies, for all my ways are before Thee, O Lord.

Let my supplication draw nigh before Thee, O Lord; according to Thine oracle give me understanding.

Let my petition come before Thee, O Lord; according to Thine oracle deliver me.

My lips shall pour forth a hymn when Thou hast taught me Thy statutes.

My tongue shall speak of Thy sayings, for all Thy commandments are righteousness.

Let Thy hand be for saving me, for I have chosen Thy commandments.

I have longed for Thy salvation, O Lord, and Thy law is my meditation.

175 My soul shall live and shall praise Thee, and Thy judgments will help me.

I have gone astray like a sheep that is lost; O seek Thy servant, for I have not forgotten Thy commandments.

Glory. Both now. Alleluia.

THE EIGHTEENTH KATHISMA

PSALM CXIX. 119
An ode of ascents.

UNTO the Lord in mine affliction have I cried, and He heard me.

O Lord, deliver my soul from unrighteous lips and from a crafty tongue.

What shall be given unto thee and what shall be added unto thee for thy crafty tongue?

The arrows of the mighty one, sharpened with coals of the desert.

5 Woe is me, for my sojourning is prolonged; I have tented with the tentings of Kedar, my soul hath long been a sojourner.

With them that hate peace I was peaceable; when I spake unto them, they warred against me without a cause.

PSALM CXX. 120
An ode of ascents.

I HAVE lifted up mine eyes to the mountains, from whence cometh my help.

My help cometh from the Lord, Who hath made heaven and the earth.

Give not thy foot unto moving, and may He not slumber that keepeth thee.

Behold, He shall not slumber nor shall He sleep, He that keepeth Israel.

5   The Lord shall keep thee; the Lord is thy shelter at thy right hand.

The sun shall not burn thee by day, nor the moon by night.

The Lord shall keep thee from all evil, the Lord shall guard thy soul.

The Lord shall keep thy coming in and thy going out, from henceforth and for evermore.

PSALM CXXI. 121

An ode of ascents.

I WAS glad because of them that said unto me: Let us go into the house of the Lord.

Our feet have stood in thy courts, O Jerusalem.

Jerusalem is builded as a city which its dwellers share in concord.

For there the tribes went up, the tribes of the Lord, as a testimony for Israel, to give thanks to the Name of the Lord.

5   For there are set thrones unto judgment, thrones over the house of David.

Ask now for the things which are for the peace of Jerusalem, and for the prosperity of them that love thee.

Let peace be now in thy strength, and prosperity in thy palaces.

For the sake of my brethren and my neighbours, I spake peace concerning thee.

Because of the house of the Lord our God, I have sought good things for thee.

PSALM CXXII. 122

An ode of ascents.

UNTO Thee have I lifted up mine eyes, unto Thee that dwellest in heaven.

Behold, as the eyes of servants look unto the hands of their masters, as the eyes of the handmaid look unto the hands of her mistress, so do our eyes look unto the Lord our God, until He take pity on us.

Have mercy on us, O Lord, have mercy on us, for greatly are we filled with abasement.

Greatly hath our soul been filled therewith; let reproach come upon them that prosper, and abasement on the proud.

PSALM CXXIII. 123

An ode of ascents.

HAD it not been that the Lord was with us, let Israel now say, had it not been that the Lord was with us,

When men rose up against us, then had they swallowed us up alive.

When their wrath raged against us, then had the water overwhelmed us.

Our soul hath passed through a torrent; then had our soul passed through the water that is irresistible.

Blessed be the Lord Who hath not given us to be a prey to their teeth.

Our soul like a sparrow was delivered out of the snare of the hunters.

The snare is broken, and we are delivered.

Our help is in the Name of the Lord, Who hath made heaven and the earth.

>Glory. Both now. Alleluia.

PSALM CXXIV. 124

An ode of ascents.

THEY that trust in the Lord shall be as Mount Sion; he that dwelleth at Jerusalem, nevermore shall he be shaken.

Mountains are round about her, and the Lord is round about His people from henceforth and for evermore.

For the Lord will not permit the rod of sinners to be upon the lot of the righteous, lest the righteous stretch forth their hands unto iniquities.

Do good, O Lord, unto them that are good and unto the upright of heart.

5 But them that turn aside unto crooked ways shall the Lord lead away with the workers of iniquity; peace be upon Israel.

PSALM CXXV. 125

An ode of ascents.

WHEN the Lord turned again the captivity of Sion, we became as men that are comforted.

Then was our mouth filled with joy, and our tongue with rejoicing.

Then shall they say among the nations: The Lord hath done great things unto them.

The Lord hath done great things among us, and we are become glad.

5 Turn again, O Lord, our captivity, like streams in the south.

They that sow with tears shall reap with rejoicing.

In their going they went, and they wept as they cast their seeds.

But in their coming shall they come with rejoicing, bearing their sheaves.

PSALM CXXVI. 126
An ode of ascents.

EXCEPT the Lord build the house, in vain do they labour that build it.

Except the Lord guard the city, in vain doth he watch that guardeth her; it is vain for you to rise at dawn.

Ye that eat the bread of sorrow, rouse yourselves after resting, when He hath given sleep to His beloved.

Lo, sons are the heritage of the Lord, the reward of the fruit of the womb.

5 Like arrows in the hand of a mighty man, so are the sons of them that were outcasts.

Blessed is he that shall fulfil his desires with them; they shall not be put to shame when they speak to their enemies in the gates.

PSALM CXXVII. 127

An ode of ascents.

BLESSED are all they that fear the Lord, that walk in His ways.

Thou shalt eat the fruit of thy labours; blessed art thou, and well shall it be with thee.

Thy wife shall be as a fruitful vine on the sides of thy house,

Thy sons like young olive trees round about thy table.

5 Behold, so shall the man be blessed that feareth the Lord.

The Lord bless thee out of Sion, and mayest thou see the good things of Jerusalem all the days of thy life.

And mayest thou see thy children's children; peace be upon Israel.

PSALM CXXVIII. 128

An ode of ascents.

MANY a time have they warred against me from my youth, let Israel now say,

Many a time have they warred against me from my youth, and yet they have not prevailed against me.

The sinners wrought upon my back, they lengthened out their iniquity.

The Lord is righteous; He hath cut asunder the necks of sinners.

5 Let them be put to shame and turned back, all they that hate Sion.

Let them be as the grass upon the housetops, which before it is plucked up is withered away.

Wherefore the reaper filleth not his hand, nor he that gathereth sheaves his bosom.

Nor have they that passed by said: The blessing of the Lord come upon you; we have blessed you in the Name of the Lord.

Glory. Both now. Alleluia.

PSALM CXXIX. 129
An ode of ascents.

O UT of the depths have I cried unto Thee, O Lord; O Lord, hear my voice.

Let Thine ears be attentive to the voice of my supplication.

If Thou shouldest mark iniquities, O Lord, O Lord, who shall stand? For with Thee there is forgiveness.

For Thy Name's sake have I patiently waited for Thee, O Lord; my soul hath waited patiently for Thy word, my soul hath hoped in the Lord.

5 From the morning watch until night, from the morning watch let Israel hope in the Lord.

For with the Lord there is mercy, and with Him is plenteous redemption; and He shall redeem Israel out of all his iniquities.

PSALM CXXX. 130
An ode of ascents.

O LORD, my heart is not exalted, nor are mine eyes become lofty.

Nor have I walked in things too great or too marvellous for me.

If I were not humble-minded but exalted my soul, as one weaned from his mother, so wouldst Thou requite my soul.

Let Israel hope in the Lord, from henceforth and for evermore.

PSALM CXXXI. 131
An ode of ascents.

REMEMBER, O Lord, David and all his meekness.

How he made an oath unto the Lord, and vowed unto the God of Jacob:

I shall not go into the dwelling of my house, I shall not ascend upon the bed of my couch,

I shall not give sleep to mine eyes, nor slumber to mine eyelids, nor rest to my temples,

5 Until I find a place for the Lord, a habitation for the God of Jacob.

Lo, we have heard of it in Ephratha, we have found it in the plains of the wood.

Let us go forth into His tabernacles, let us worship at the place where His feet have stood.

Arise, O Lord, into Thy rest, Thou and the ark of Thy holiness.

Thy priests shall be clothed with righteousness, and Thy righteous shall rejoice.

10 For the sake of David Thy servant, turn not Thy face away from Thine anointed one.

The Lord hath sworn in truth unto David, and He will

not annul it: Of the fruit of thy loins will I set upon thy throne.

If thy sons keep My covenant and these testimonies which I will teach them,

Their sons also shall sit for ever on thy throne.

For the Lord hath elected Sion, He hath chosen her to be a habitation for Himself.

15 This is My rest for ever and ever; here will I dwell, for I have chosen her.

Blessing, I will bless her pursuit; her beggars will I satisfy with bread.

Her priests will I clothe with salvation, and her saints with rejoicing shall rejoice.

There will I make to spring forth a horn for David, I have prepared a lamp for My Christ.

His enemies will I clothe with shame, but upon Him shall My sanctification flourish.

PSALM CXXXII. 132

An ode of ascents.

BEHOLD now, what is so good or so joyous as for brethren to dwell together in unity?

It is like the oil of myrrh upon the head, which runneth down upon the beard, upon the beard of Aaron, which runneth down to the fringe of his raiment.

It is like the dew of Aermon, which cometh down upon the mountains of Sion.

For there the Lord commanded the blessing, life for evermore.

PSALM CXXXIII. 133

An ode of ascents.

BEHOLD now, bless ye the Lord, all ye servants of the Lord.

Ye that stand in the house of the Lord, in the courts of the house of our God,

In the nights lift up your hands unto the holies, and bless the Lord.

The Lord bless thee out of Sion, He that made heaven and the earth.

Glory. Both now. Alleluia.

THE NINETEENTH KATHISMA

PSALM CXXXIV. 134

Alleluia.

PRAISE ye the Name of the Lord; O ye servants, praise the Lord.

Ye that stand in the house of the Lord, in the courts of the house of our God,

Praise ye the Lord, for the Lord is good; chant unto His Name, for it is good.

For the Lord hath chosen Jacob unto Himself, Israel for His own possession.

For I know that the Lord is great, and that our Lord is above all gods.

All that the Lord hath willed He hath done, in heaven and on the earth, in the seas and in all the abysses.

Bringing clouds up from the uttermost parts of the earth, lightnings for the rain hath He made.

He bringeth winds out of His treasuries; He smote the firstborn of Egypt, from man unto beast.

He sent forth signs and marvels in the midst of thee, O Egypt, on Pharaoh and on all his servants.

He smote many nations and slew mighty kings.

Seon, king of the Amorites, and Og, king of the land of Basan, and all the kingdoms of Canaan.

And He gave their land for an inheritance, an inheritance for Israel His people.

O Lord, Thy Name endureth for ever, and Thy memorial unto generation and generation.

For the Lord will judge His people, and because of His servants shall He be comforted.

15 The idols of the nations are silver and gold, the works of the hands of men.

They have a mouth but shall not speak, eyes have they and shall not see.

Ears have they and shall not hear, nor is there any breath in their mouth.

Let those that make them become like unto them, and all they that put their trust in them.

O house of Israel, bless ye the Lord. O house of Aaron, bless ye the Lord. O house of Levi, bless ye the Lord.

20 Ye that fear the Lord, bless ye the Lord.

Blessed is the Lord out of Sion, Who dwelleth in Jerusalem.

PSALM CXXXV. 135

Alleluia.

O GIVE thanks unto the Lord, for He is good; for His mercy endureth for ever.

O give thanks unto the God of gods; for His mercy endureth for ever.

O give thanks unto the Lord of lords; for His mercy endureth for ever.

To Him Who alone hath wrought great wonders; for His mercy endureth for ever.

5 To Him that made the heavens with understanding; for His mercy endureth for ever.

To Him that established the earth upon the waters; for His mercy endureth for ever.

To Him Who alone hath made great lights; for His mercy endureth for ever.

The sun for dominion of the day; for His mercy endureth for ever.

The moon and the stars for dominion of the night; for His mercy endureth for ever.

To Him that smote Egypt with their firstborn; for His mercy endureth for ever.

And led forth Israel out of the midst of them; for His mercy endureth for ever.

With a strong hand and a lofty arm; for His mercy endureth for ever.

To Him that divided the Red Sea into parts; for His mercy endureth for ever.

And led Israel through the midst thereof; for His mercy endureth for ever.

And overthrew Pharaoh and his host in the Red Sea; for His mercy endureth for ever.

To Him that led His people through the wilderness; for His mercy endureth for ever.

To Him that smote great kings; for His mercy endureth for ever.

And slew mighty kings; for His mercy endureth for ever.

Seon, king of the Amorites; for His mercy endureth for ever.

And Og, king of the land of Basan; for His mercy endureth for ever.

And gave their land for an inheritance; for His mercy endureth for ever.

An inheritance for Israel His servant; for His mercy endureth for ever.

For in our humiliation the Lord remembered us; for His mercy endureth for ever.

And redeemed us from our enemies; for His mercy endureth for ever.

He that giveth food to all flesh; for His mercy endureth for ever.

O give thanks unto the God of heaven; for His mercy endureth for ever.

PSALM CXXXVI. 136

For David. By Jeremias, in the captivity.

By the waters of Babylon, there we sat down and we wept when we remembered Sion.

Upon the willows in the midst thereof did we hang our instruments.

For there, they that had taken us captive asked us for words of song.

And they that had led us away asked us for a hymn, saying: Sing us one of the songs of Sion.

How shall we sing the Lord's song in a strange land?

If I forget thee, O Jerusalem, let my right hand be forgotten.

Let my tongue cleave to my throat, if I remember thee not,

If I set not Jerusalem above all other, as at the head of my joy.

Remember, O Lord, the sons of Edom, in the day of Jerusalem,

10   Who said: Lay waste, lay waste to her, even to the foundations thereof.

O daughter of Babylon, thou wretched one, blessed shall he be who shall reward thee wherewith thou hast rewarded us.

Blessed shall he be who shall seize and dash thine infants against the rock.

> Glory. Both now. Alleluia.

PSALM CXXXVII. 137
David's. Of Aggeus and Zacharias.

I WILL confess Thee, O Lord, with my whole heart; and before angels will I chant unto Thee, for Thou hast heard all the words of my mouth.

I will worship towards Thy holy temple and confess Thy Name, for Thy mercy and for Thy truth; for Thou hast magnified Thy holy Name above all that is.

In whatsoever day I call upon Thee, quickly hearken unto me; Thou shalt abundantly endow my soul with Thy strength.

Let all the kings of the earth, O Lord, confess Thee, for they have heard all the words of Thy mouth.

5   And let them sing in the ways of the Lord, for great is the glory of the Lord.

For the Lord is exalted, yet on lowly things He looketh; and things haughty He knoweth from afar.

Though I should walk in the midst of affliction, Thou shalt quicken me; against the wrath of mine enemies hast Thou stretched forth Thy hands, and Thy right hand hath saved me.

The Lord shall give recompense in my behalf. O Lord, Thy mercy endureth for ever; disdain not the work of Thy hands.

PSALM CXXXVIII. 138

For the end. David's. A psalm of Zacharias in the dispersion.

O LORD, Thou hast proved me and Thou knowest me; Thou knowest my down-sitting and mine up-rising.

Thou hast discerned my thoughts from afar; my path and my lot hast Thou traced out,

And hast foreseen all my ways, for there is no guile in my tongue.

Behold, Lord, Thou knowest all things, the last and the first; Thou hast fashioned me and hast laid Thy hand upon me.

Thy knowledge is too wonderful for me; it is mighty, I cannot attain unto it.

Whither shall I go from Thy Spirit? And from Thy presence whither shall I flee?

If I go up into heaven, Thou art there; if I go down into hades, Thou art present there.

If I take up my wings toward the dawn, and make mine abode in the uttermost parts of the sea,

Even there shall Thy hand guide me, and Thy right hand shall hold me.

And I said: Surely darkness shall tread me down, and the night shall be turned into light in my delight.

For darkness will not be darkness with Thee, and night shall be bright as the day; as is the darkness thereof, even so shall the light thereof be.

For Thou hast possessed my reins; O Lord, Thou hast holpen me from my mother's womb.

I will confess Thee, for awesomely art Thou wondrous; marvellous are Thy works, and my soul knoweth it right well.

My bone is not hid from Thee, which Thou madest in secret; nor my substance in the nethermost parts of the earth.

15 My being while it was still unformed Thine eyes did see, and in Thy book shall all men be written; day by day they are formed, when as yet there be none of them.

But to me, exceedingly honourable are Thy friends, O Lord; their principalities are made exceeding strong.

I will count them, and they shall be multiplied more than the sand; I awoke and I am still with Thee.

Surely Thou wilt slay the sinners, O God. Ye men of blood, depart from me.

For Thou wilt say concerning their thoughts that in vain shall they take Thy cities.

20 As for them that hate Thee, O Lord, have I not hated them? And because of Thine enemies have I not pined away?

With perfect hatred have I hated them; they are reckoned enemies with me.

Prove me, O God, and know my heart; examine me and know my paths.

And see if the way of iniquity be in me, and guide me in the way everlasting.

PSALM CXXXIX. 139

For the end. A psalm of David.

RESCUE me, O Lord, from the evil man; from the unjust man deliver me.

Who have devised injustice in their heart; all the day long have they arrayed themselves for wars.

They have whetted their tongue like that of a serpent; the venom of asps is under their lips.

Keep me, O Lord, from the hand of the sinner; rescue me from unjust men who have devised to undermine my steps.

5 The proud have hid a snare for me, and with cords have they spread a snare for my feet; stumbling-blocks near the paths have they set for me.

I said unto the Lord: Thou art my God; give ear, O Lord, unto the voice of my supplication.

Lord, O Lord, Thou strength of my salvation, Thou hast overshadowed my head in the day of battle.

Because of my desire, O Lord, give me not up unto the sinner. They have taken counsel against me; forsake me not, lest they should be exalted.

As for the head of those that encircle me, the mischief of their lips shall cover them.

10 Coals shall fall upon them; in fire shalt Thou cast them down, and they shall not stand in afflictions.

A babbling man shall not prosper on the earth; evils shall hunt an unjust man to his destruction.

I know that the Lord will maintain the cause of the poor and the justice of the paupers.

Surely the righteous shall confess Thy Name, and the upright shall dwell in Thy presence.

Glory. Both now. Alleluia.

PSALM CXL. 140
A psalm of David.

LORD, I have cried unto Thee, hearken unto me; attend to the voice of my supplication when I cry unto Thee.

Let my prayer be set forth as incense before Thee, the lifting up of my hands as an evening sacrifice.

Set, O Lord, a watch before my mouth, and a door of enclosure round about my lips.

Incline not my heart unto words of evil, to make excuse with excuses in sins,

With men that work iniquity; and I will not join with their chosen.

The righteous man will chasten me with mercy and reprove me; as for the oil of the sinner, let it not anoint my head.

For yet more is my prayer in the presence of their pleasures; swallowed up near by the rock have their judges been.

They shall hear my words, for they be sweetened; as a clod of earth is broken upon the earth, so have their bones been scattered nigh unto hades.

For unto Thee, O Lord, O Lord, are mine eyes, in Thee have I hoped; take not my soul away.

Keep me from the snare which they have laid for me,

and from the stumbling-blocks of them that work iniquity.

The sinners shall fall into their own net; I am alone until I pass by.

PSALM CXLI. 141

Instruction by David, when he was in the cave praying.

WITH my voice unto the Lord have I cried, with my voice unto the Lord have I made supplication.

I will pour out before Him my supplication, mine affliction before Him will I declare.

When my spirit was fainting within me, then Thou knewest my paths.

In this way wherein I have walked they hid for me a snare.

5 I looked upon my right hand, and beheld, and there was none that did know me.

Flight hath failed me, and there is none that watcheth out for my soul.

I have cried unto Thee, O Lord; I said: Thou art my hope, my portion art Thou in the land of the living.

Attend unto my supplication, for I am brought very low.

Deliver me from them that persecute me, for they are stronger than I.

10 Bring my soul out of prison that I may confess Thy Name.

The righteous shall wait patiently for me until Thou shalt reward me.

PSALM CXLII. 142

David's. When his son Abessalom pursued him.

O LORD, hear my prayer, give ear unto my supplication in Thy truth; hearken unto me in Thy righteousness.

And enter not into judgment with Thy servant, for in Thy sight shall no man living be justified.

For the enemy hath persecuted my soul; he hath humbled my life down to the earth.

He hath sat me in darkness as those that have been long dead, and my spirit within me is become despondent; within me my heart is troubled.

5 I remembered days of old, I meditated on all Thy works, I pondered on the creations of Thy hands.

I stretched forth my hands unto Thee; my soul thirsteth after Thee like a waterless land.

Quickly hear me, O Lord; my spirit hath fainted away.

Turn not Thy face away from me, lest I be like unto them that go down into the pit.

Cause me to hear Thy mercy in the morning; for in Thee have I put my hope.

10 Cause me to know, O Lord, the way wherein I should walk; for unto Thee have I lifted up my soul.

Rescue me from mine enemies, O Lord; unto Thee have I fled for refuge. Teach me to do Thy will, for Thou art my God.

Thy good Spirit shall lead me in the land of uprightness; for Thy Name's sake, O Lord, shalt Thou quicken me.

In Thy righteousness shalt Thou bring my soul out of affliction, and in Thy mercy shalt Thou utterly destroy mine enemies.

And Thou shalt cut off all them that afflict my soul, for I am Thy servant.

Glory. Both now. Alleluia.

THE TWENTIETH KATHISMA

PSALM CXLIII. 143

David's. Concerning Goliath.

Blessed is the Lord my God, Who teacheth my hands for battle and my fingers for war.

My mercy and my refuge, my helper and my deliverer,

My defender is He; and in Him have I hoped, Who subjected my people under me.

O Lord, what is man, that Thou art made known unto him? Or the son of man, that Thou takest account of him?

Man is like unto vanity, his days like a shadow pass away.

O Lord, bow down the heavens and come down; touch the mountains, and they shall smoke.

Flash forth lightning, and Thou shalt scatter them; send forth Thine arrows, and Thou shalt trouble them.

Send forth Thy hand from on high; rescue and deliver me from many waters, from the hand of the sons of aliens,

Whose mouth hath spoken vanity; and their right hand is the right hand of unrighteousness.

O God, a new song shall I sing unto Thee; with the psaltery of ten strings shall I chant unto Thee,

Who givest salvation unto kings, Who redeemest David Thy servant from the evil sword.

Deliver me and rescue me from the hand of the sons of aliens whose mouth hath spoken vanity, and their right hand is the right hand of unrighteousness,

Whose sons are like new plants, strongly planted in their youth,

Their daughters prettified, and lavishly adorned like unto a temple.

15 Their garners are full, bursting forth with all manner of store.

Their sheep are abundant in young, multiplying in their gateways; their oxen are fat.

There is no breach of wall, nor any passage, nor any outcry in their streets.

They have called the people blessed which fareth thus; but blessed is the people whose God is the Lord.

PSALM CXLIV. 144

David's. A psalm of praise.

I WILL exalt Thee, O my God, my king, and I will bless Thy Name for ever, yea, for ever and ever.

Every day will I bless Thee, and I will praise Thy Name for ever, yea, for ever and ever.

Great is the Lord and exceedingly to be praised, and of His greatness there is no end.

Generation and generation shall praise Thy works, and Thy power shall they declare.

5 Of the majesty of the glory of Thy holiness shall they speak, and they shall tell of Thy wonders.

And the power of Thine awesome deeds shall they relate, and they shall tell of Thy majesty.

The memory of the multitude of Thy goodness shall they pour forth, and in Thy righteousness shall they rejoice.

Compassionate and merciful is the Lord, long-suffering and plenteous in mercy.

The Lord is good to all, and His compassions are over all His works.

Let all Thy works, O Lord, give praise to Thee, and let Thy righteous ones bless Thee.

Of the glory of Thy kingdom shall they speak, and shall tell of Thy dominion,

To make Thy dominion known to the sons of men, and the glory of the majesty of Thy kingdom.

Thy kingdom is the kingdom of all the ages, and Thy sovereignty is in every generation and generation.

Faithful is the Lord in all His words, and holy in all His works.

The Lord upholdeth all that are falling, and setteth up all that are broken down.

The eyes of all look to Thee with hope, and Thou givest them their food in due season.

Thou openest Thy hand and fillest every living thing with Thy favour.

Righteous is the Lord in all His ways, and holy in all His works.

The Lord is nigh unto all that call upon Him, to all that call on Him in truth.

The will of them that fear Him shall He do, and their supplication shall He hear, and He shall save them.

The Lord preserveth all that love Him, but all the sinners shall He utterly destroy.

My mouth shall speak the praise of the Lord, and let all flesh bless His holy Name, for ever, yea, for ever and ever.

Glory. Both now. Alleluia.

PSALM CXLV. 145
Alleluia. Of Aggeus and Zacharias.

PRAISE the Lord, O my soul. I will praise the Lord in my life, I will chant unto my God for as long as I have my being.

Trust ye not in princes, in the sons of men, in whom there is no salvation.

His spirit shall go forth, and he shall return unto his earth.

In that day all his thoughts shall perish.

5 Blessed is he of whom the God of Jacob is his help, whose hope is in the Lord his God,

Who hath made heaven and the earth, the sea and all that is therein,

Who keepeth truth unto eternity, Who executeth judgment for the wronged, Who giveth food unto the hungry.

The Lord looseth the fettered; the Lord maketh wise the blind; the Lord setteth aright the fallen; the Lord loveth the righteous; the Lord preserveth the proselytes.

He shall adopt for His own the orphan and widow, and the way of sinners shall He destroy.

10 The Lord shall be king unto eternity; thy God, O Sion, unto generation and generation.

PSALM CXLVI. 146
Alleluia. Of Aggeus and Zacharias.

PRAISE ye the Lord, for a psalm is a good thing; let praise be sweet unto our God.

The Lord buildeth up Jerusalem, He shall gather together the dispersed of Israel.

He healeth the broken in heart and bindeth their fractures together.

He numbereth the multitude of the stars and calleth them all by name.

5 Great is our Lord, and great is His strength, and of His understanding there is no measure.

The Lord lifteth up the meek, but humbleth sinners to the earth.

Begin your song to the Lord with thanksgiving, chant unto God with the harp,

To Him that covereth heaven with clouds, Who prepareth rain for the earth,

Who maketh grass to grow on the mountains, and green herb for the service of man,

10 Who giveth to the beasts their food, and to the younglings of the ravens which call upon Him.

He shall not delight in the strength of a horse, nor in the legs of man is He well pleased.

The Lord is well pleased in them that fear Him, and in them that hope in His mercy.

PSALM CXLVII. 147
Alleluia. Of Aggeus and Zacharias.

PRAISE the Lord, O Jerusalem; praise thy God, O Sion.

For He hath strengthened the bars of thy gates, He hath blessed thy sons within thee.

He bringeth peace upon thy borders, and with the fatness of the wheat He filleth thee.

He sendeth His saying unto the earth; right swiftly runneth His word.

He giveth His snow like wool; the mist He sprinkleth like ashes.

He hurleth His ice like morsels. Who shall stand before His cold?

He shall send forth His word and melt them; His wind shall blow and the waters shall flow.

He declareth His word unto Jacob, His statutes and judgments to Israel.

He hath not dealt so with every nation, nor hath He shown His judgments unto them.

> Glory. Both now. Alleluia.

PSALM CXLVIII. 148

Alleluia. Of Aggeus and Zacharias.

PRAISE the Lord from the heavens, praise Him in the highest.

Praise Him, all ye His angels; praise Him, all ye His hosts.

Praise Him, O sun and moon; praise Him, all ye stars and light.

Praise Him, ye heavens of heavens, and thou water that art above the heavens.

Let them praise the Name of the Lord; for He spake, and they came to be; He commanded, and they were created.

He established them for ever, yea, for ever and ever; He hath set an ordinance, and it shall not pass away.

Praise the Lord from the earth, ye dragons, and all ye abysses,

Fire, hail, snow, ice, blast of tempest, which perform His word,

The mountains and all the hills, fruitful trees, and all cedars,

The beasts and all the cattle, creeping things and winged birds,

Kings of the earth, and all peoples, princes and all the judges of the earth,

Young men and virgins, elders with the younger; let them praise the Name of the Lord, for exalted is the Name of Him alone.

His praise is above the earth and heaven, and He shall exalt the horn of His people.

This is the hymn for all His saints, for the sons of Israel, and for the people that draw nigh unto Him.

PSALM CXLIX. 149

Alleluia.

SING unto the Lord a new song; His praise is in the church of the saints.

Let Israel be glad in Him that made him, let the sons of Sion rejoice in their King.

Let them praise His Name in the dance; with the timbrel and the psaltery let them chant unto Him.

For the Lord taketh pleasure in His people, and He shall exalt the meek with salvation.

The saints shall boast in glory, and they shall rejoice upon their beds.

The high praise of God shall be in their throat, and two-edged swords shall be in their hands,

To do vengeance among the heathen, punishments among the peoples,

To bind their kings with fetters, and their nobles with manacles of iron,

To do among them the judgment that is written. This glory shall be to all His saints.

PSALM CL. 150
Alleluia.

PRAISE ye God in His saints, praise Him in the firmament of His power.

Praise Him for His mighty acts, praise Him according to the multitude of His greatness.

Praise Him with the sound of trumpet, praise Him with the psaltery and harp.

Praise Him with timbrel and dance, praise Him with strings and flute.

5 Praise Him with tuneful cymbals, praise Him with cymbals of jubilation. Let every breath praise the Lord.

Glory. Both now. Alleluia.

A PSALM

This psalm is one written by David's own hand, though it is not numbered with the one hundred and fifty psalms. Composed when he fought in single combat with Goliath.

I was the smallest among my brethren, and the youngest in the house of my father; I did shepherd the sheep of my father.

My hands made an instrument, and my fingers fashioned a psaltery.

And who shall tell my Lord? The Lord Himself, He Himself shall hearken.

He sent forth His angel and took me from the flocks of my father, and anointed me with the oil of His anointing.

5   My brethren were big and good, yet the Lord took not pleasure in them.

I went forth to meet the alien, and he cursed me by his idols.

But I drew his own sword and beheaded him, and took away the reproach from the sons of Israel.

THE NINE ODES

THE FIRST ODE

An Ode of Moses in the Exodus
(Exodus 15:1–19)

When he had utterly drowned Pharaoh in the deep, Moses said:
To the Lord let us sing, for gloriously is He glorified.

LET us sing to the Lord, for gloriously is He glorified; horse and rider hath He hurled into the sea.

A helper and protector was He unto me for salvation. This is my God, and I will glorify Him; the God of my father, and I will exalt Him.

The Lord quenching wars, Lord is His Name.

The chariots of Pharaoh and his hosts He hurled into the sea; the chosen mounted captains He plunged into the Red Sea.

With the open sea He covered them; they sank into the deep like a stone.

Thy right hand, O Lord, is glorified in strength; Thy right hand, O Lord, hath shattered enemies, and in the multitude of Thy glory hast Thou ground down the adversaries.

Thou sentest forth Thy wrath; it consumed them like stubble.

And at the breath of Thy wrath, the water parted asunder; the waters were hardened like a wall, hardened also were the waves in the midst of the sea.

The enemy said: I will pursue, I will overtake, I will divide the spoil, I will satisfy my soul, I will destroy with my sword; my right hand shall have dominion.

Thou sentest forth Thy breath; the sea covered them; they sank like lead in the turbulent water.

Who is like unto Thee among the gods, O Lord? Who is like unto Thee? Glorified in holies, wonderful in glories, doing marvels.

Thou hast stretched forth Thy right hand; the earth swallowed them up.

Thou hast guided by Thy righteousness this Thy people whom Thou hast redeemed; Thou hast called them by Thy strength into Thy holy habitation.

The nations heard and waxed wroth; pangs took hold of them that dwell in Philistia.

For 8 verses

Then did the rulers of Edom hasten, and the princes of the Moabites; trembling took hold of them, all the dwellers in Canaan melted away.

Let fear and trembling fall upon them; by the greatness of Thine arm, let them be made like unto stone,

For 6 verses

Until Thy people pass over, O Lord, until they pass over, even this Thy people which Thou didst take for Thine own.

Bring them in and plant them in the mountain of Thine inheritance, in Thy prepared habitation which Thou hast fashioned, O Lord, even the sanctuary which Thy hands have prepared.

For 4 verses

The Lord is king of the ages, yea, for ever and evermore.

For the horse of Pharaoh with chariots and riders went into the sea, and the Lord brought upon them the water of the sea; but the sons of Israel walked through dry land in the midst of the sea.

Glory. Both now.

THE SECOND ODE

It should be noted that the Second Ode is never chanted, save only in the Great Fast during which, on Tuesday only, it is chanted to its end. And for each of the troparia of the Second Ode of the Canon, we say:
Glory to Thee, our God, glory to Thee.

An Ode of Moses in the Deuteronomy
(Deuteronomy 32:1–43)

After the Law had been written, again an Ode of Moses.

ATTEND, O heaven, and I will speak, and let the earth hear the words of my mouth.

Let mine instruction be awaited like rain, and let my words come down like the dew, like a shower upon the tender grass, like snow upon the green herb,

For I have called upon the Name of the Lord. Render majesty unto our God.

As for God, His works are true, and all His ways are judgments.

God is faithful, and there is no unrighteousness in Him; righteous and holy is the Lord.

They have sinned; blameworthy children are not His.

O generation crooked and perverse, are these the recompenses ye pay to the Lord?

This is a people foolish and not wise; did not He Himself, thy Father, take thee for His own, and make thee, and fashion thee?

Remember the days of old, consider now the years of generations and generations.

Ask thy father, and he will declare unto thee; thine elders, and they will tell thee.

10 When the Most High divided the nations, when He scattered abroad the sons of Adam, He set the boundaries of nations according to the number of the angels of God.

And there was made a portion for the Lord, Jacob His people; the line of His inheritance was Israel.

He filled him with abundance in the wilderness, in the thirsting of heat in a waterless land; He led him about and instructed him, and kept him as the apple of His eye.

As an eagle would shelter his nest and hath yearned for his nurslings, and spreading his wings hath received them, and hath taken them upon his pinions,

So the Lord alone led them, and there was no strange god among them.

15 He brought them up on the strength of the land, He fed them with the increase of the fields.

He suckled them with honey from a rock, and with oil out of the solid rock,

With butter of cows and milk of sheep, with fat of lambs and rams, of sons of bulls and he-goats, with the fat of kidneys of wheat; and they drank wine, the blood of the grape.

And Jacob ate and was filled; and the beloved one kicked, he grew fat, he grew thick, he waxed broad, and he forsook God Who had made him, and departed from God his Saviour.

They provoked Me with strange gods, and with their abominations they embittered Me.

20 They sacrificed to demons, and not to God; to gods, whom they knew not; new and recent gods were come, which their fathers knew not.

Thou hast abandoned the God Who begat thee, and hast forgotten God Who feedeth thee.

And the Lord saw and was jealous, and He was provoked by the wrath of His sons and daughters.

And He said: I will turn My face away from them, and I will show what shall come upon them in the last days; for it is a perverse generation; sons, in whom there is no faith.

They have made Me jealous with that which is not god, they have angered Me with their idols; and I will provoke them to jealousy with that which is no nation, with a foolish nation will I provoke them to wrath.

25 For a fire is kindled out of My wrath, it shall burn unto nethermost hades; I shall devour them and the land and the increase thereof; it shall set on fire the foundations of the mountains.

I will gather evils upon them, I will perfect Mine arrows against them.

They shall melt away in famine and the devouring of birds, the bending down of their backs shall be incurable; teeth of wild beasts shall I send forth against them, along with the wrath of things that creep upon the earth.

From without, the sword shall bereave them of children, and out of their inner chambers shall issue fear. The young man shall perish with the maiden, the suckling with him that long hath been old.

I said: I would scatter them, I would make their memorial to cease from among men,

Were it not for the wrath of their enemies, yea, lest their adversaries should live long and unite to set upon them,

Lest they should say: Our own high hand, and not the Lord, hath done all these things.

For it is a nation that hath lost counsel, and there is no understanding in them; they have not the wit to understand all these things.

Let them admit in a time that is to come:

How shall one man pursue a thousand, and how shall two put to flight tens of thousands, if God had not yielded them up and the Lord surrendered them?

For their gods are not as our God; and our enemies are void of understanding.

For out of the vines of Sodom is their vine, and their vine-branch out of Gomorrha; their grape is a grape of gall, it is a cluster of bitterness to them.

The rage of dragons is their wine, and the incurable wrath of asps.

Lo, are not all these things stored up with Me and sealed among My treasures?

In the day of vengeance I will requite, in the moment when their foot stumbleth; for nigh is the day of their perdition. And the things prepared for you are at hand.

For the Lord shall judge His people, and because of His servants shall He be comforted.

For He saw that they were palsied, and had failed in their invasion, and that they were enfeebled.

And the Lord said: Where are their gods in whom they trusted?

The fat of whose sacrifices ye ate, and ye drank the wine of their libations? Let them arise, and let them help you; let them be your protectors.

Behold, behold, I am; and there is no god beside Me. I will slay, and I will make to live; I will smite, and I will heal; and there is none who shall deliver out of My hands.

For unto heaven I will lift up My hand, and I will swear by My right hand and I will say: I live unto eternity.

For I will sharpen My sword like lightning, and My hand shall take hold of judgment; I will render justice unto Mine enemies, and them that hate Me will I recompense.

I will make Mine arrows drunk with blood, and My sword shall feed on flesh, on the blood of wounded men and of captivity, from the head of the princes of the enemy.

Be glad with Him, O ye heavens, and let all the angels of God worship Him.

Be glad, ye nations, with His people, and let all the sons of God be strengthened in Him; for the blood of His sons shall He avenge, and He shall judge and execute vengeance upon His enemies; and to them that hate Him shall He render their due, and the Lord shall purify the land of His people.

Glory. Both now.

THE THIRD ODE

A Prayer of Hannah, the Mother of Samuel the Prophet
(1 Kings 2:1–10)

The barren one strangely beareth a son and praiseth God:
Holy art Thou, O Lord, and Thee my spirit praiseth.

My heart is established in the Lord, my horn is exalted in my God, my mouth is enlarged over mine enemies, I am glad in Thy salvation.

For there is none holy as the Lord, for there is none righteous as our God, and there is none holy beside Thee.

Boast ye not, and utter not high things unto excess, nor let boastful words of pride come forth from your mouth.

For the Lord is a God of knowledge, and a God that prepareth His own ways.

5 The bow of the mighty is become weak, and the strengthless have girded themselves with power.

They that were full of bread are sunk into low estate, and the hungry have been rested in the land; for the barren hath borne seven, and she that abounded in children is enfeebled.

The Lord slayeth and engendereth life, He bringeth down to hades and bringeth up again.

The Lord maketh poor and enricheth, He bringeth low and lifteth high again.

He raiseth the pauper from the earth, and from the dunghill doth He lift up the poor man to seat him with the mighty of the people, and He maketh him heir of their throne of glory.

For 8 verses

He granteth his prayer to him that prayeth, and hath blest the years of the righteous man.

For the mighty man shall not be strong in his own strength; the Lord will weaken his adversary; the Lord is holy.

For 6 verses

Let not the wise man boast in his wisdom, let not the mighty man boast in his might, let not the rich man boast in his riches;

But in this let him that boasteth make his boast, that he hath understanding and knoweth the Lord, and that He worketh judgment and righteousness in the midst of the earth.

For 4 verses

The Lord hath gone up into the heavens and hath thundered; He will judge the ends of the earth, for He is righteous.

And He will give strength to our kings, and He will lift up the horn of His anointed one.

Glory. Both now.

THE FOURTH ODE

A Prayer of Abbacum the Prophet
(Abbacum 3:2–19)

Do thou declare, O Abbacum, the Word's kenosis.
Glory be to Thy power, O Lord.

O LORD, I have heard Thy report, and I was afraid; O Lord, I considered Thy works, and I was amazed.

Between two living creatures shalt Thou be known; when the years draw nigh, Thou shalt be acknowledged; when the season cometh, Thou shalt be shown forth; when my soul is troubled, in Thine anger shalt Thou remember mercy.

God shall come out of Thaeman, and the Holy One out of a mountain overshadowed and densely wooded.

His virtue hath covered the heavens, and the earth was full of His praise.

And His brightness shall be as the light; horns are in His hands, and He hath established a mighty love of His strength.

Before His face shall the Word proceed, and He shall go forth for instruction at His feet.

He stood, and the earth was shaken; He beheld, and the nations melted away.

The mountains were violently burst asunder, the everlasting hills melted away at His everlasting going forth.

Because of troubles, I looked upon the tents of the Ethiopians; even the tabernacles of the land of Madiam were dismayed.

10   Nay, with the rivers wast Thou wroth, O Lord? Nay, against the rivers was Thine anger, or against the sea Thine attack? For Thou shalt mount upon Thy horses, and Thy chariots are salvation.

Bending Thy bow, Thou shalt bend it against sceptres; the Lord saith: The land of rivers shall be rent asunder.

They shall see Thee, and the people shall be in travail, while Thou scatterest the courses of the waters; the abyss gave forth her voice and raised her form on high.

Lifted up was the sun, and the moon stood still in her course; at the light shall Thy missiles go forth, at the brilliance of the gleam of Thy weapons.

With threatening shalt Thou diminish the earth, and with anger shalt Thou trample down nations.

15   Thou wentest forth for the salvation of Thy people, to save Thine anointed ones art Thou come. Thou didst cast death upon the heads of transgressors, Thou didst lay fetters upon their neck at the end.

Thou hast cut asunder with fury the heads of the mighty; they shall quake within themselves, they shall break open their bridles, like the poor man that eateth in secret.

And Thou hast mounted Thy horses in the sea, and they trouble the many waters.

I kept watch, and my belly was troubled at the voice of the prayers of my lips; and trembling went into my bones, and within me my strength was troubled.

I will rest in the day of mine affliction, that I may go up to the people of my sojourning.

For 8 verses

20   For the fig tree shall not bear fruit, and there shall be no increase for the vines;

The labour of the olive shall fail, and the plains shall bear no food.

For 6 verses

The sheep have failed from their grazing, and there are no oxen at the cribs.

But as for me, in the Lord will I be glad, I will rejoice in God my Saviour.

For 4 verses

The Lord is my God and my might, and He will instruct my feet unto perfection.

25   He mounteth me on high, that I might be victor with His song.

      Glory. Both now.

THE FIFTH ODE

A Prayer of Esaias the Prophet
(Esaias 26:9–20)

Esaias' prophecy, which is also his prayer.
O Lord our God, grant us peace.

Out of the night my spirit waketh at dawn unto Thee, O God, for Thy commandments are a light upon the earth.

Learn righteousness, ye that dwell upon the earth.

For the ungodly man hath come to an end; every man that learneth not righteousness on the earth shall not execute truth; let the ungodly man be taken away, that he may not see the glory of the Lord.

O Lord, lofty is Thine arm, and they knew it not; but when they know it, let them be put to shame.

5 Zeal shall lay hold upon an uninstructed people, and now fire shall devour the adversaries.

O Lord our God, bestow Thy peace upon us; for Thou hast given all things unto us.

O Lord our God, take us for Thy possession. O Lord, besides Thee we know none other; we call upon Thy Name.

But the dead shall not see life, nor shall physicians raise them up; therefore hast Thou brought wrath upon them and hast slain them, and hast taken every male of them away.

Add more evils upon them, O Lord; add more evils upon them that are glorious upon the earth.

10 O Lord, in tribulation we remembered Thee; in a small affliction was Thine instruction with us.

For 8 verses

And as a woman in travail cometh to her time for giving birth, and because of her travail she crieth out, so have we become in the presence of Thy beloved one.

Because of fear of Thee, O Lord, have we conceived and suffered pangs, and given birth to the spirit of Thy salvation, which we have wrought on the earth.

For 6 verses

We shall not fail, but all they shall fail that dwell upon the earth.

The dead shall rise, and they that are in the tombs shall awake, and they that be in the earth shall rejoice.

For 4 verses

For the dew which Thou sendest is healing for them, but the land of the ungodly shall perish.

Go, my people; enter thine inner chamber, shut thy door, hide thyself for a little while, until the wrath of the Lord shall pass away.

Glory. Both now.

THE SIXTH ODE

A Prayer of Jonas the Prophet
(Jonas 2:3–10)

As Thou didst the Prophet Jonas save, save us also, O Lord.
From out of the sea monster Jonas cried aloud and said:

I CRIED aloud in mine affliction unto the Lord my God, and He hearkened unto me; out of the womb of hades Thou heardest my cry and my voice.

Thou hast cast me off into the depths of the heart of the sea, and the floods encompassed me.

All Thy billows and Thy waves passed over me.

For 8 verses

And I said: I am banished from the sight of Thine eyes; shall I indeed look again toward Thy holy temple?

Water is poured out about me even unto my soul, the uttermost abyss surrounded me; my head hath gone down into the clefts of the mountains, I went down into the earth whose bars are everlasting barriers.

For 6 verses

Yet, let my life come up out of corruption unto Thee, O Lord my God.

When my soul was fainting within me, I remembered the Lord; yea, let my prayer come unto Thee, even unto Thy holy temple.

For 4 verses

They that observe vain and false things have abandoned mercy for themselves.

But as for me, with the voice of praise and thanksgiving will I sacrifice unto Thee; whatsoever I have vowed for my salvation, I will pay unto Thee, O Lord.

Glory. Both now.

THE SEVENTH ODE

A Prayer of the Holy Three Children
(Daniel 3:26–56)

The praise of the Three Youths doth quench the flame.
O our God and the God of our Fathers, blessed art Thou.

BLESSED art Thou, O Lord, the God of our Fathers, and praised and glorified is Thy Name unto the ages.

For righteous art Thou in all which Thou hast done for us; and all Thy works are true, and upright are Thy ways, and all Thy judgments are true.

And judgments of truth hast Thou performed in all things which Thou hast brought upon us, and upon the holy city of our fathers, Jerusalem; for in truth and judgment hast Thou brought all these things upon us for our sins.

For we have sinned and have transgressed in departing from Thee, and all things wherein we have greatly sinned; and Thy commandments have we not heard, nor have we given heed, nor done as Thou hast enjoined us, that it might go well with us.

And all that Thou hast done to us, and all that Thou hast brought upon us, in judgment that is true hast Thou done them; and Thou hast surrendered us into the hands of lawless enemies, of most hateful apostates, and to a king that is unjust and the most wicked in all the earth.

And now we are not able to open our mouth; shame and reproach are we become for Thy servants and for them that revere Thee.

Deliver us not up utterly, for Thy holy Name's sake, neither disannul Thou Thy covenant, and cause not Thy mercy to depart from us, for Abraham's sake, Thy beloved, and for Isaac's sake, Thy servant, and for Israel's, Thy holy one,

To whom Thou didst say that Thou wouldst multiply their seed, as the stars of heaven and as the sand on the shore of the sea.

For, O Sovereign Master, we are become the least of all the nations, and are humbled in all the earth this day because of our sins.

And there is not at this time any prince, nor prophet, nor leader, nor whole-burnt offering, nor sacrifice, nor oblation, nor incense, nor place to bring first fruits before Thee and to find mercy.

But in a contrite soul and in a spirit of humility may we be accepted.

As in whole-burnt offerings of rams and bullocks, and in tens of thousands of fat lambs, so let our sacrifice be acceptable before Thee this day, and let it be performed hereafter before Thee; for there is no shame to them that trust in Thee.

Yea, now we follow Thee with our whole heart, and we fear Thee, and we seek Thy face; O put us not to shame.

But deal with us according to Thy tenderness and according to the multitude of Thy mercy.

Rescue us according to Thy wondrous works, and give glory to Thy Name, O Lord.

And let all them be confounded that show evils to Thy servants, and let them be put to shame and be deprived of all their power, and let the strength of them be shattered.

And let them know that Thou art Lord, the only God, and glorious throughout the whole world.

And the king's servants, which had cast them in, ceased not from heating the furnace with naphtha, and pitch, and tow, and wood of the vine.

And the flame poured out above the furnace nine and forty cubits, and it broke through and enveloped in flames those of the Chaldeans which it found around the furnace.

20 But the Angel of the Lord came down to be with Azarias and those that were with him in the furnace, and He drave the flame of the fire out of the furnace.

And He made the midst of the furnace like a whistling wind that beareth dew, and the fire touched them not at all, nor brought any grief, nor troubled them.

Then the three, as out of a single mouth, praised and blessed and glorified God in the furnace saying:

The Hymn of the Three, Which the Youths Sang
For 8 verses

Blessed art Thou, O Lord, the God of our Fathers, and supremely praised and supremely exalted unto the ages.

And blessed is the holy Name of Thy glory, which is supremely praised and supremely exalted unto the ages.

For 6 verses

25 Blessed art Thou in the temple of Thy holy glory, Thou Who art supremely praised and supremely exalted unto the ages.

Blessed art Thou that lookest upon the abysses, that sittest upon the Cherubim, Thou Who art supremely praised and supremely exalted unto the ages.

For 4 verses

Blessed art Thou upon the throne of the glory of Thy kingdom, Thou Who art supremely praised and supremely exalted unto the ages.

Blessed art Thou in the firmament of the heaven, Thou Who art supremely praised and supremely exalted unto the ages.

Glory. Both now.

THE EIGHTH ODE

The Hymn of the Holy Three Children
(Daniel 3:57–88)

O praise the Lord, ye creatures which He hath made.
O praise ye the Lord, ye works of His, and supremely
exalt Him unto all the ages.

Bless the Lord, all ye works of the Lord:
O praise ye the Lord and supremely exalt Him unto the ages.

Bless the Lord, ye angels of the Lord, and ye heavens of the Lord:
O praise ye the Lord and supremely exalt Him unto the ages.

Bless the Lord, all ye waters above the heavens, and all ye powers of the Lord:
O praise ye the Lord and supremely exalt Him unto the ages.

Bless the Lord, O sun and moon, and ye stars of heaven:
O praise ye the Lord and supremely exalt Him unto the ages.

5 Bless the Lord, every rain and dew, and all ye winds:
> O praise ye the Lord and supremely exalt Him unto the ages.

Bless the Lord, fire and heat of burning, winter cold and summer heat:
> O praise ye the Lord and supremely exalt Him unto the ages.

Bless the Lord, O falls of dew and snow, O ice and cold:
> O praise ye the Lord and supremely exalt Him unto the ages.

Bless the Lord, O hoar frosts and snows, O lightnings and clouds:
> O praise ye the Lord and supremely exalt Him unto the ages.

Bless the Lord, O light and darkness, O nights and days:
> O praise ye the Lord and supremely exalt Him unto the ages.

10 Bless the Lord, O earth, mountains and hills, and all things that spring up therein:
> O praise ye the Lord and supremely exalt Him unto the ages.

Bless the Lord, O fountains, seas and rivers, O monsters of the sea, and all things that move in the waters:
> O praise ye the Lord and supremely exalt Him unto the ages.

For 8 verses

Bless the Lord, all ye winged creatures of the sky, O beasts and all cattle:
> O praise ye the Lord and supremely exalt Him unto the ages.

Bless the Lord, ye sons of men; let Israel bless the Lord:
> O praise ye the Lord and supremely exalt Him unto the ages.

For 6 verses

Bless the Lord, ye priests of the Lord, ye servants of the Lord:
> O praise ye the Lord and supremely exalt Him unto the ages.

15 Bless the Lord, ye spirits and ye souls of the righteous, ye saints, and ye that be humble of heart:
> O praise ye the Lord and supremely exalt Him unto the ages.

For 4 verses

Bless the Lord, O Ananias, Azarias, and Misael:
> O praise ye the Lord and supremely exalt Him unto the ages.

Bless the Lord, ye Apostles, Prophets, and Martyrs of the Lord:
> O praise ye the Lord and supremely exalt Him unto the ages.

We bless Father, Son, and Holy Spirit, the Lord:
> We praise the Lord and supremely exalt Him unto the ages.
> Both now and ever, and unto the ages of ages. Amen.

We praise, we bless, and we worship the Lord:
> Praising the Lord and supremely exalting Him unto the ages.

THE NINTH ODE

The Song of the Theotokos
(Luke 1:46–55)

Her Son and God doth the maiden Mother praise.
With hymns let us magnify the Theotokos.

My soul doth magnify the Lord, and my spirit hath rejoiced in God my Saviour.

For He hath looked upon the lowliness of His handmaiden; for behold, from henceforth all generations shall call me blessed.

For the Mighty One hath done great things to me, and holy is His Name; and His mercy is on them that fear Him unto generation and generation.

He hath showed strength with His arm, He hath scattered the proud in the imagination of their heart.

He hath put down the mighty from their seat, and exalted them of low degree; He hath filled the hungry with good things, and the rich He hath sent empty away.

He hath holpen His servant Israel in remembrance of His mercy, as He spake to our fathers, to Abraham and his seed for ever.

The Prayer of Zacharias, the Father of the Forerunner
(Luke 1:68–79)

Zacharias blesseth the birth of his son.

Blessed be the Lord God of Israel, for He hath visited and wrought redemption for His people,

And hath raised up a horn of salvation for us in the house of His servant David,

As He spake by the mouth of His holy ones, the prophets of old,

THE NINTH ODE

That we should be saved from our enemies, and from the hand of all that hate us,

To deal mercifully with our fathers, and to remember His holy covenant,

For 8 verses

The oath which He sware to our father Abraham, that He would grant unto us that we be delivered out of the hand of our enemies,

That we might serve Him without fear, in holiness and righteousness before Him all the days of our life.

For 6 verses

And thou, child, shalt be called the prophet of the Most High; for thou shalt go before the face of the Lord, to prepare His ways,

To give knowledge of salvation unto His people, by the remission of their sins, through the bowels of mercy of our God,

For 4 verses

Whereby the Dayspring from on high hath visited us, to give light to them that sit in darkness and in the shadow of death,

To guide our feet into the way of peace.

Glory. Both now.

THE END
AND TO OUR GOD BE GLORY.

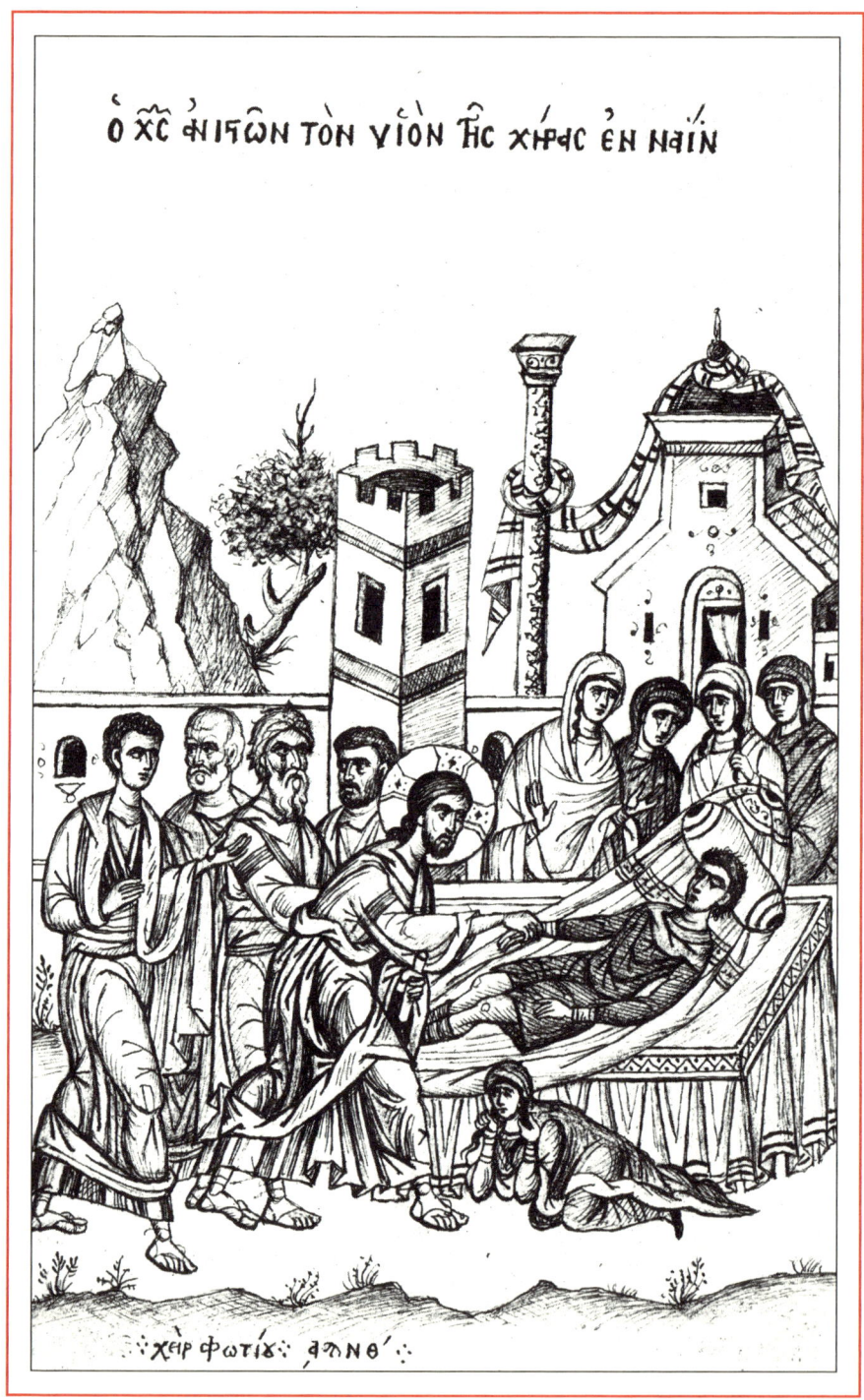

CHRIST RESURRECTING THE SON OF THE WIDOW OF NAIN

A PRAYER FOR THE REPOSED

When an Orthodox Christian has reposed, it is traditional to read the entire Psalter over him during the wake which precedes the funeral. This prayer is recited on his behalf at the end of each kathisma.

Lord, have mercy. (12)

REMEMBER, O Lord our God, Thy servant our brother (sister) *Name,* departed in the faith and hope of eternal life, and since Thou art good and the Friend of man, Who forgivest sins and overlookest iniquities: remit, pardon, and forgive all his (her) transgressions, both voluntary and involuntary; deliver him (her) from eternal torment and the fire of Gehenna, and grant unto him (her) to partake of and enjoy Thine everlasting good things, prepared for them that love Thee. If he (she) hath sinned, yet he (she) hath not forsaken Thee, and hath believed firmly in Thee, God the Father, the Son, and the Holy Spirit glorified in Trinity; and he (she) hath in Orthodox manner confessed the Unity in Trinity and the Trinity in Unity even unto his (her) last breath. Therefore be merciful unto him (her) and receive his (her) faith in Thee in place of works; and since Thou art compassionate grant him (her) rest with Thy Saints, for no man can live and not sin; but Thou alone art without sin, and Thy righteousness is unto the ages; for Thou alone art a God of mercies and compassion and love for man, and to Thee do we send up glory, to the Father, and to the Son, and to the Holy Spirit, now and ever, and unto the ages of ages. Amen.

ORDER OF READING THE PSALTER (KATHISMATA)

1) *Outside Great Lent:*

Day	Matins	Vespers
Su	II, III [a]	
M	IV, V	VI
Tu	VII, VIII	IX
W	X, XI	XII
Th	XIII, XIV	XV
F	XIX, XX	XVIII
Sa	XVI, XVII	I

[a] The Psalter is not read at Sunday Vespers, nor on the feasts of the Lord when there is a Vigil. On Sundays for the third kathisma of Matins, the Seventeenth Kathisma is read, or if there is a Vigil or celebrated Saint, the polyeleos is chanted. If there should be a Vigil or celebrated Saint on other days of the week, the polyeleos (Pss. 134, 135) is chanted with the selection of psalmic verses from the Eclogarion proper to the feast.

2) *During the First, Second, Third, Fourth, and Sixth Weeks of Great Lent:*

Day	Matins	Hours				Vespers
		First	Third	Sixth	Ninth	
Su	II, III b					
M	IV, V, VI		VII	VIII	IX	XVIII
Tu	X, XI, XII	XIII	XIV	XV	XVI	XVIII
W	XIX, XX, I	II	III	IV	V	XVIII
Th	VI, VII, VIII	IX	X	XI	XII	XVIII
F	XIII, XIV, XV		XIX	XX		XVIII
Sa	XVI, XVII					I

3) *During the Fifth Week of Great Lent:*

Day	Matins	Hours				Vespers
		First	Third	Sixth	Ninth	
Su	II, III b					
M	IV, V, VI		VII	VIII	IX	X
Tu	XI, XII, XIII	XIV	XV	XVI	XVIII	XIX
W	XX, I, II	III	IV	V	VI	VII
Th	VIII		IX	X	XI	XII
F	XIII, XIV, XV		XIX	XX		XVIII
Sa	XVI, XVII					I

b In the Greek usage, the Seventeenth Kathisma (Ps. 118) is read or the polyeleos is chanted, as may be appointed.

4) *When the Feast of the Annunciation Falls on the Thursday of the Fifth Week of Great Lent,* the Great Canon is chanted on the Tuesday of that Week, and the Psalter is read as follows:

Day	Matins	Hours				Vespers
		First	Third	Sixth	Ninth	
Su	II, III, XVII					
M	IV, V, VI	VII	VIII	IX	X	XI
Tu	XII		XIII	XIV	XV	XVI
W	XIX, XX, I	II	III	IV	V	
Th	VI, VII, VIII c	IX	X	XI	XII	
F	XIII, XIV, XV		XIX	XX		XVIII
Sa	XVI, XVII					I

c On Thursday, the Feast of the Annunciation, the polyeleos (Ps. 44) is chanted at the third kathisma of Matins.

5) *During Holy Week:* d

Day	Matins	Hours				Vespers
		First	Third	Sixth	Ninth	
Su	II, III b					
M	IV, V, VI		VII	VIII		XVIII
Tu	IX, X, XI		XII	XIII		XVIII
W	XIV, XV, XVI		XIX	XX		XVIII
Th						
F						
Sa	XVII					

d The Psalter is not read from Holy and Great Thursday until the evening of Saturday of Renewal (or Bright) Week, when it is resumed at Vespers.

Every Kathisma is divided into three *stases;* after each of the first two *stases* the following is said:

Glory to the Father, and to the Son, and to the Holy Spirit; both now and ever, and unto the ages of ages. Amen.

Alleluia, Alleluia, Alleluia. Glory to Thee, O God. (*Thrice*)

Lord, have mercy. (*Thrice*)

Glory to the Father, and to the Son, and to the Holy Spirit; both now and ever, and unto the ages of ages. Amen.

But at the end of the whole Kathisma:

Glory to the Father, and to the Son, and to the Holy Spirit; both now and ever, and unto the ages of ages. Amen.

Alleluia, Alleluia, Alleluia. Glory to Thee, O God. (*Twice*)

Alleluia, Alleluia, Alleluia. Glory to Thee, O God our Hope, O Lord, glory be to Thee.

NUMBERING OF THE PSALMS

Septuagint	Hebrew (KJ)
1–8	1–8
9	9–10
10–112	11–113
113	114–115
114	116 v. 1–9
115	116 v. 10–19
116–145	117–146
146	147 v. 1–11
147	147 v. 12–20
148–150	148–150

The numbering of the Kathismata is the same in both the Hebrew and the Septuagint versions, however the psalms within the Kathismata vary.

PSALMS ASSIGNED TO THE SERVICES[†]
(Septuagint numbering)

Vespers:	Ps. 103 (Sunset Psalm), Pss. 140, 141, 129, 116, 122; and, during Great Lent and on fastdays before the meal in the refectory, Pss. 33, 144.
Great Compline:	Pss. 4, 6, 12, 24, 30, 90, 50, 101, 69, 142.
Small Compline:	Pss. 50, 69, 142.
Midnight Service:	—Weekdays: Ps. 50, Kathisma XVII, Pss. 120, 133. —Saturday: Ps. 50, Kathisma IX, Pss. 120, 133. —Sunday: Ps. 50.
Matins:	Pss. 19, 20, the Six Psalms (3, 37, 62, 87, 102, 142), Ps. 50, the Nine Odes, Pss. 148, 149, 150.[‡]
First Hour:	Pss. 5, 89, 100.
Mid-hour of 1st:	Pss. 45, 91, 92.
Third Hour:	Pss. 16, 24, 50.
Mid-hour of 3rd:	Pss. 29, 31, 60.
Sixth Hour:	Pss. 53, 54, 90.
Mid-hour of 6th:	Pss. 55, 56, 69.
Ninth Hour:	Pss. 83, 84, 85.
Mid-hour of 9th:	Pss. 112, 137, 139.
Typica:	Pss. 102, 145, 33.
Panagia or refectory:	Pss 144, 121.

[†] See also charts above on the order of reading the Psalter.
[‡] For many holy days, the polyeleos is chanted. See Glossary, under *Polyeleos*.

GLOSSARY

ECLOGARION A selection of verses from the Psalter appropriate to the feast.

KATHISMA (pl. *kathismata*) Each of the twenty sections into which the Psalter is divided. Also a short troparion, chanted or read during Matins at the end of each kathisma from the Psalter.

MID-HOUR A short service recited between each of the ordinary Hours, and similar to them in structure.

PANAGIA A small *prosphoron* (loaf of bread) offered and elevated in honour of the Mother of God, the *All-Holy One (Panagia)*. The ceremony is accompanied by a short service of prayers and psalms, and is performed in the refectory. The bread is then distributed among the community.

POLYELEOS A term applied primarily to Psalms 134 and 135, and to certain psalmic verses from the *Eclogarion* chanted after the first two readings of the kathismata in Matins on certain feast-days. In the Greek usage, Psalm 44 is the polyeleos for the feasts of the Mother of God. Also on the three Sundays immediately preceding the beginning of Lent, Psalm 136 is added to the polyeleos.

PROKEIMENON Verses, usually from the Psalter, chanted immediately before the scriptural prophecies, the Epistle reading in the Liturgy, and the Gospel reading in Matins on feast-days and Sundays. Also chanted daily after the hymn, "O Joyous Light" in Vespers.

SIX PSALMS The psalms read daily at the beginning of Matins (Pss. 3, 37, 62, 87, 102, 142). There should be no movement or noise in church while they are being read, and all are required to remain standing. Only at the beginning and at the end of the reading of the Six Psalms do the faithful make the sign of the Cross, never during them, not even during the doxology and Alleluia after the first three psalms.

TYPICA A short service consisting of psalms, hymns, and prayers taken from the Divine Liturgy and chanted on days when the Liturgy is not celebrated. In modern practice, the Typica is read on the eves of the Nativity and Theophany even though there is a Liturgy, and it is also read when there is a Liturgy of the Presanctified Gifts.

The Psalter

was typeset in Adobe Caslon by the Holy Transfiguration
Monastery and printed in an edition of 5000 copies by
Friesens in Altona, Manitoba, on Rolland Opaque,
sixty pound weight, an acid-free paper
of proven durability.

GLORY BE TO GOD FOR ALL THINGS. AMEN